THE COMMON CROSS

THE
COMMON
CROSS

JOHN S. KENNEDY

NEW YORK

McMULLEN BOOKS, INC.

Nihil Obstat:

JOHN BYRNES
Censor Librorum

Imprimatur:

✠HENRY J. O'BRIEN, D.D.
Archbishop of Hartford

January 25, 1954

Library of Congress Catalogue Card Number: 54-7090

Copyright 1954
McMULLEN BOOKS, INC.
Printed in the U. S. A.

CONTENTS

For My Sister Elizabeth

FOREWORD

Everything in the life and utterance of Christ has a bearing on the commonplace details of our experience. In our pain and perplexities, especially, we cannot do better than go to the New Testament for light. A sentence, an action, a gesture by the Saviour shows us in a flash what our course must be. A few words from St. Paul's racing pen link an incident in our life with one in the life of Christ. A single verse, in Gospel or Epistle, leaps from the page and strikes home to the heart, in reproach or direction or encouragement.

In the following pages some few details of Christ's last days are examined for the instruction and example they afford us in situations as trying as they are familiar. Excerpts from St. Paul's Letters are used both for their clarification of the Gospels and their appositeness to our own problems. The point aimed at is this: the crosses appointed for us are not individual and several; they are so many aspects of the common cross, first borne by Christ, then by the members of the Mystical Body.

THE COMMON CROSS

1

LONELINESS

There is an aspect of the Passion which we may
have slighted: the loneliness of Christ as He went
the distance of this ordeal. No one except our
Lady understood what it was all about, what it
was for, what would be its issue, what its effects.
And she was not with Him throughout it. During
most of it she was parted from Him. Those who
encompassed His death were arrayed in icy enmity
against Him, their hearts turned away from the
sun of His love. His Apostles faltered in faith, in
understanding, in courage. In a real and terrible
sense He was utterly alone. And being truly, in-
tensely human, He knew tormenting loneliness.

It is the lonely Christ who, at the Last Supper,
speaks eloquently, feelingly, of the union of Christ
and the Christian, and bestows on the Christian
the means of union with Him. That first Holy
Thursday, when the darkness of night enwrapped
the Holy City, the darkness of malice enwrapped

the souls of those polishing their plans for His destruction, the darkness of misunderstanding enwrapped the minds of His own, He gathered His little company of chosen ones to Him in the hushed, lamplit upper room. There He took His leave of them. But first, He celebrated the Pasch, the most solemn religious observance of the old dispensation of law which was passing away. And then He celebrated the most solemn religious observance of the new dispensation of love which was being ushered in. He instituted the Mass, the Eucharist, the priesthood.

The Mass, the Eucharist, the priesthood have this in common: they make possible Christ's union with the Christian in an altogether special manner and degree. In ordaining priests He was taking selected men into Himself, making them sharers in His office and powers in a way which the most daring imagination could never have anticipated, enabling those with holy orders to bring and to be Christ to humanity in all subsequent ages. In giving the Mass He was making possible the limitless extension, unto the last bounds of earth and time, of Calvary's Sacrifice, so that people in all places might directly participate, identified with Victim and Priest, in the great Act of redemption and reconciliation. In giving the Eucharist He was communicating Himself to poor wayfaring mortals as daily food and drink and a perpetual living

Presence. Henceforth, no one conversant with His doings this night could think of God as remote, aloof, unreachable. Rather, He was to be knit to men in the most intimate and vital union.

To point the meaning of these breath-taking gifts, He spoke to the Apostles before braving the storm of betrayal, agony, death. He in His loneliness discoursed to them in their loneliness of the fusion of Him and His which would rout all loneliness. In a figure of rarest beauty and poignancy He developed at length the very core and crown of His whole teaching: that Christ lives in the Christian, that the Christian lives in Christ, that one and the same life is shared by the Christian and Christ.

"I am the vine," He told them; "you are the branches. Abide in me and I in you. I have chosen you and appointed you that you should bear fruit and that your fruit should remain. He who abides in me, and I in him, he bears much fruit. Without me you can do nothing. As the branch cannot bear fruit of itself unless it remain on the vine, so neither can you unless you abide in me. If anyone does not abide in me, he shall be cast aside as a branch and wither and . . . shall be thrown into the fire and shall burn. My Father is the vine-dresser. Every branch in me that bears no fruit, he will take away; and every branch that bears fruit he will cleanse that it may bear more fruit."

believe in Him that Christ gives the power to become one with Him. Faith is the bridge by which we pass from the isolation and meanness of our several merely natural selves to plenary identification with our blessed Lord. Increase of faith speeds and solidifies our growth in His likeness.

We have faith. Let us cherish it. Let us protect and nourish it. It is precious; it is also perishable. We are lost without it; we can all too easily lose it. We live in a world which lacks it, scorns it, vigorously opposes it. From all sides, in a hundred disarming guises, there swarm upon us ideas, opinions, suggestions, aims irreconcilable with it. Hence, the absolute and primary necessity of safeguarding and fostering our faith and that of our children. If our faith can diminish, it can also increase.

Secondly, *we must strive to make our lives agree in every particular with Christ*. That is not to say that we must imitate the circumstances and details of His earthly life, which would be in every case impossible; rather, that we must seek "to harmonize (our) thoughts, affections, aspirations with those of the Lord . . . to think with Him, to feel with Him, to judge with Him, to see with His eyes (hear with His ears), and speak with His tongue."

To this end we must familiarize ourselves with His life, reading and rereading the Gospels, immersing ourselves in them. If only we give it a try, we shall find this the most fascinating and rewarding of all the reading we have ever done. We can, for example, read and meditate a chapter of the Gospels a day, after supper, or before our night prayers, or whenever the best opportunity occurs. The Gospels give us Christ in the majesty of His divinity and the winsomeness of His humanity. From them we shall learn the secret, the patterns, of His thought and action—His simplicity, His humility, His obedience, His poverty, His suffering; His attitude toward the poor, toward sinners, toward His enemies; His patience, His compassion, His forgiveness, His love of His native land, His prayer, His zeal—these and scores of other points upon which we can and must bring ourselves into accord with Him.

Thirdly, *we must make proper and profitable use of the Mass and the sacraments.*

We can so easily fall into, and stay in, the habit of being merely externally present at Mass, of wool-gathering, or worrying, or staring about with ferret-eyed curiosity or fish-eyed vacancy, or half-heartedly rattling off a jumble of prayers, or flipping through a missal without concentration—in all of these failing to keep in touch with the world-shaking mystery taking place at the altar. There must possess us a lively awareness that the Sacrifice of the Cross is being renewed, that the oblation by which our ransoming was wrought is being repeated, that the Son of God is—here and now, within our reach, where the candle shine gilds the snowy cloth—being immolated. The purpose of this extension of Calvary's action to our parish church, whether grand or humble, is that we may be drawn into it, take part in it, act ourselves.

Our doing so is, of course, the most potent means of our transformation in Christ, especially if we receive Holy Communion. Then do we share the consummation of the Sacrifice, then are we most effectively taken into it, do we most effectively take it into ourselves. Hence, we must be alive to the meaning of the Mass; we must go to Mass as often as we possibly can (not as a duty grudgingly or automatically met, but as an incomparable opportunity of growth); we must be active participants in it, not passive spectators at it; we must receive the slain Victim that His death may work its wonders, His life its planting of the seeds of glory, in us.

Confession, too, furthers our union with Christ. We ought not to regard it as simply a stop at a service station for the wiping clean of a spotted windshield. It is not meant to be just a way of getting back to where we were before we committed this sin or that. No, it is intended as a means of steady spiritual advance, of ever closer assimilation to Christ, by the elimination of habits of sin, the tearing out of certain root-faults, the correction of imperfections, the rubbing away of blemishes, which are a rejection or an abuse of grace. The confessional is not merely a dumping ground for our spiritual rubbish; it is a place where we mature in grace, come step by step nearer to the divine Ideal. We should so regard it: our resort to it should be more frequent, our preparation for it more painstaking, our use of it more positive.

Fourthly, we are the more deeply and securely plunged into Christ *the more fully we are at one with His Church*. It is the Church which links us to Christ, blends us into Christ. It imparts faith in Him and love of Him at baptism, restores or adds to His grace in confession, brings us His very Self in the Mass and the Eucharist. Nor is it merely an agency for distributing these, a conveyor belt transmitting them, a storehouse where they may be secured. It is not something one resorts to in need, then proceeds independent of. It is the Mystical Body of Christ.

Membership in it means, as St. Paul puts it, that "you are no longer exiles or aliens. The saints are your fellow citizens. You belong to God's household. Apostles and prophets are the foundation on which you are built, and the chief cornerstone of it is Jesus Christ Himself. In Him the whole fabric is bound together . . . In Him you too are being built in with the rest, so that God may find in you

21

a dwelling place for His Spirit." To think with the
Church, to judge with the Church, to stand with
the Church, to move with the Church is to be in
exact accord with Christ. But this is impossible if
our contact with the Church is casual, superficial,
intermittent, if we stand off from it, are cool or
censorious to it, if for us the Church is no more
than a club where we occasionally drop in, rather
than a corporate entity of which we are united
members.

Who could have conceived of such dignity for
us paltry beings—that we are fused with Christ?
Beside this splendid reality, how wretchedly windy
seems all the florid talk about the common man,
the average man, the man in the street, the prole-
tarian, the citizen of the world. Whether patroniz-
ing or pretentious, equally empty. We are the
branches of the true vine—when God the Father
sees us, He sees Christ His dearly beloved. Poor
though we are, sadly limited, unprepossessing,
sickly, untalented, undistinguished, unimportant,
unwanted—we are the members of the Son of God.

At one with Him, how can we be lonely? Every
breath we take is shared with Him; every action
we perform is weighted with His worth; in every
movement, at every moment, we are companioned
by the Lord of Lords. In us the fire-shining angels
salute Him, the illustrious saints surround Him.
He is in us; we are in Him.

And in Him we are in profound communion with all who are His. As the same stream of life circulates through the branches of the common vine, so the same stream of love circulates through the branches of the Christian vine, vivifying all, merging all in charity. We pray for one another, merit for one another, suffer for one another. Nor are our dead who died in Christ lost to us. Indeed, they are more immediately at one with us than ever before, because they are caught up to Christ in the beatific vision. They read our hearts and know our needs as never before; they obtain for us the helps we require for better assimilation to the Saviour whose immediate presence they have entered.

How, in view of all this, can we lead mediocre lives, invertebrate lives, yawning or playing or frittering or grubbing our years away? How can we be satisfied with what is tawdry and trivial, with the flashy, the ephemeral, the tinsel treasures which rust and moth eat away? We have a vocation immeasurably beyond that. We are chosen and appointed that we may bear fruit, fruit that remains—the fruit of virtue, the fruit of high holiness, the fruit of Christlike impact on others. There is no such thing as working at this vocation part time, or half-fulfilling it. We throw ourselves into it unreservedly, or we are thrown away unreservedly. We are of the vine or we are not of the vine. "My Father is the vine-dresser," says Christ, and He closely watches the vine. "Every branch in me that bears no fruit, he will take away; and every branch that bears fruit he will cleanse that it may bear more fruit." That cleansing comes, as we shall see, in the form of trials, reverses, suffering, grief; it is healthful, it increases the yield of grace.

We must carry out that vocation, we must live on the level to which we are called. Only so do we progress toward "that maturity which is . . . the completed growth of Christ."

2

FEAR AND GUILT

After speaking so luminously of the bond between Himself and the Christian, Christ goes from
the upper room to the hillside garden. We must
not think of His agony there as primarily a physical ordeal. True, there are unmistakable physical
evidences of Christ's acute suffering—the prostra-
tion, the trembling, the groaning, the sweat of
blood. Yet these are but effects. They merely indi-
cate the intensity of the crisis of the spirit through
which the Saviour passes. Torture from without is
to come on the morrow; what He is now undergoing is torture from within.

He had more than once told the Apostles of the
fact and manner of His life's coming to an end.
Only this evening, at the supper table become an
altar, He had announced that the time was at
hand for this to be accomplished. When He led
them from the cenacle, it was to meet the fate He
had predicted. He begged them to keep vigil with

Him, to watch and pray as He wrestled with His weighty sorrow and called on His Father.

And their response? They huddle under the stone wall, near the tree trunks, gather their cloaks around them against the sharp night air of early spring, and fall asleep. Repeatedly He pleads with them not to leave Him alone; each time, consternation gives away to lassitude and they steal away from Him in slumber. His Father now seems withdrawn from Him; His Mother is at a distance, somewhere in the city.

This Passion of His, what will it mean to those for whom it will be undergone? He will endure it for the redemption of all men without exception. But how many will pay it little heed, no heed. How many will ignore it, be indifferent to it, fail to profit by it, or actually misuse it to their further incrimination. Is it worth while? There are spiritual writers who tell us that in this harsh hour beneath the olives Christ sees hell, and at the sight a storm of grief rushes through His being.

There are two factors on which we should dwell further. The first is the sense of fear, and the second is the sense of guilt.

Fear grips and rips Christ in Gethsemane. He is vividly aware that He is to be put through a succession of agonies—the scourging of His body, the shredding of His brow by thorns, the grueling journey beneath the cross, the nailing of hands and feet, the suspension on the cross for creeping hours, the piercing of His side, the final desperate struggle with inexorable death. He knows it all, in advance, in detail.

And knowing it, He dreads this crescendo of suffering. He shrinks from it. "If it be possible, let this chalice pass from me." We see that He is indeed truly human, with the same revulsion from pain that we have, the same terror of its ravages, the same instinctive inclination to escape if He can. Fear shakes Christ to the core of His humanity, even as it does us.

Then there is the sense of guilt. Christ is divine, the Son of God. He is therefore indescribably sensitive to the slightest suggestion of sin. It monstrously offends Him, revolts Him, disgusts Him. For He is holiness itself, goodness itself, purity itself, and even the faintest flickering of sin galls Him.

Yet here He is loaded with all the sin of all the world, crushed with the incalculable, reeking mass of the countless crimes of mankind, from those of the first man to those of the last. They are heaped upon Him in their nauseating number and variety and stench. St. Paul does not hesitate to say that Christ, "who knew not sin," was *made* sin, *became* sin—so to speak—for our sake. That is, since He has undertaken to make reparation for the wickedness of man, He is identified with it. And His feeling of guilt, as He is engulfed in our sin, is an excruciating experience.

Turning from our scrutiny of Christ in His agony, and looking at our world and ourselves, we find that we and our contemporaries are harassed by fear and by guilt.

Fear—we could spend hours simply listing the forms which it takes today. There is fear of atomic destruction, the pulverizing of the world by weapons fantastic in their range and annihilating power. There is fear of war, involving all mankind and more horrible and devastating than any previous conflict. There is fear of Communism, enslavement to the iron depostism already riveted upon hundreds of millions and threatening to put an end to truly human history. There is fear of inflation, fear of depression, fear of solitary and destitute old age, fear of not being loved, fear of bearing children. There is fear of what people may think about us and fear that they may think nothing about us. There is fear of cancer, heart attacks, polio. You can add to the list at your leisure, rolling up a lugubrious litany of obsessive fears which rout all peace of mind and heart, and make us prey to constant and manifold anxiety.

Someone has called ours an age of anxiety, and this sums up and precisely defines our era, our lives. A thousand and one books presume to prescribe for our fears, to help us get rid of them. No two of them agree on how the task is to be done, and all of them together foster a new fear—namely, the fear of not hearing of and reading the latest book detailing the latest prescription for purging fear. But the best lesson we could have in how to handle fear is that taught us by Christ in His agony.

First, Christ fears what is real and immediate. The fear which harries Him in the garden is not prompted by chimeras or delusions, but by an actuality which is right at hand. His Passion is not a vaporous possibility, but a fact which is just about to unfold. In less than an hour the traitor's kiss will sear His cheek, the soldier's hands will pinion His arms, and then the whole torrent of horrors will riot over Him, dragging Him down to death.

We, on the other hand, lay ourselves open to punishment by fear of what might conceivably happen, what is by no means here or imminent or even probable, but merely possible. It is, of course, conceivable that almost any sort of trouble can in future overtake us; the cynic, the pessimist, says that almost every sort of trouble surely will overtake us. But carefully to catalogue them all and then plunge into an orgy of fear of the lot of them is to court insanity, if not already to evidence it. It is also, of course, to betray both a mania for total security such as no mortal has ever enjoyed and utter lack of faith in divine Providence. The point is that we have the grace to face up to, and face down, as did Christ, only those fears grounded in a concrete and present situation.

Secondly, Christ displays fortitude, exercises fortitude, conquers through fortitude. He overcomes His fear; it does not overcome Him. He is calm when His public Passion actually begins and as it mounts—calm as He is arrested, as He is insulted, as He is subjected to a mock trial, as He is struck, as He confronts Pilate, as, one by one, the major sufferings of the Passion rack Him. It is fortitude which enables Him to say now, at the end of His agony and on the verge of these pangs: "Rise up, let us go on our way"—that is, when the hour sounds, He steps bravely forth to meet His death.

This very same fortitude is ours, through the sacrament of confirmation. It is a gift of the Holy Spirit, there within us to be used. And it is equal to any contingency.

Thirdly, Christ, beset by fear, puts Himself completely in the hands of His Father. "Not my will, but thine be done." And this surrender effects not the disappearance of His fear, but the neutralizing or disarming of it. It is an impenetrable mystery, yet the fact is that His Father now somehow seems aloof from the Saviour; there is no sensible comfort, no warmth of reassurance from the thought of His Father. But He knows, nonetheless, that in the doing of His Father's will, whatever grief that may entail, are victory and peace.

It should be even so with us. No matter the sharpness and magnitude of our fear; if we will but say: "Not my will, but thine be done," then has fear lost its power to paralyze and demolish us, then is its sting drawn. God may seem distant indeed as the howling hurricane of fear dashes our heart loose from its moorings, but if we will only fix our will on His, put ourselves wholly in His hands, and cry: "Thy will be done," then we can bear, it may be with serenity and even with deep joy, the trial which impends.

As for guilt, it is curious, though not at all surprising, that at the very time when men have persuaded themselves of the non-existence of sin they are more haunted and bedeviled by an implacable sense of guilt than has ever before been the case. In the Christian ages, men were convinced of the reality of sin and were sacramentally freed of its guilt. In the post-Christian age, men are convinced of the unreality of sin and are dogged and driven mad by a guilt of which they can never get free. A sign of our times is the universal awareness of guilt, the universal obsession by guilt, the universal hunger to be liberated from guilt.

But the strange truth is that, to be quit of guilt, we must first accept it. That is, we must acknowledge that we are sinners, that we are born in sin, that again and again we have committed sin, breaking the commandments, fouling ourselves with evil, saying "No, no, no" to God and "Yes, yes, yes" to what is at odds with God, tearing ourselves away from the divine will, tearing ourselves to pieces. We must admit our sin and our sinfulness before we can get out of the maze of guilt. We must look squarely at the picture of ourselves as we really are before anything can be done about transforming us into what ideally we should be and could be.

Only when the prodigal son had said: "Father, I have sinned against heaven and before thee," could he be delivered from his sickness of heart and cease to be a ragged, famished, footsore wanderer. Speaking with all reverence, we can say that Christ in Gethsemane is a kind of divine prodigal. He has laden Himself with the hideous accumulation of our sin. As Head of the Mystical Body, He acknowledges the guilt of its members. Even as He does, the gates of heaven begin to swing open and the divine mercy to spill down upon the blasted earth.

To be delivered from the guilt which plagues us and putrefies within us, each of us must turn to God, confess and renounce his sins, and then will he be lifted up, embraced, healed, restored to the wholeness which our loving Father wills to be in us, but which we have insisted on shattering by sin. What prevents our doing so? Pride, chiefly, an inordinate self-love which refuses to face our true condition and insists on maintaining a pharisaical fiction of pristine perfection which our subconscious self is forever violently contradicting and which fissions personality.

If in our pride we deny the guilt which is hounding us, let us look at the sinless Son of God in Gethsemane. He is on the ground; He grovels; His face is in the dust. He is the very personification of humility—which means stark truthfulness. He is the very picture of contrition—which means acknowledgment of sin and breaking with sin. And when He at last gets up, the spell of fear is broken, the hold of guilt is dissipated. If we do as He did, it can be equally so with us.

3

PAIN

Before meeting Christ, Pilate evidently had thought of Him as just another crank, another of the easily forgotten trouble-makers frequently brought before him. But, subjecting the Saviour to a routine quiz, the governor is impressed by His imperturbable dignity and increasingly disturbed by the mysterious quality of His replies. He finds no offense in the prisoner and would like to release Him. Obviously, this man is no criminal, no malefactor, so why should He be punished?

But there is the roar of the crowd, coached by the Pharisees. Pilate must reckon with that. Like an implacable tide, it beats at his ears. It threatens him with the displeasure of Caesar, which would blow the governor down like a house of cards. Few are the political careerists who will not make short shrift of principle, will not sacrifice it to expediency, and Pilate is not one of that scanty company. He gropes for a way out of the impasse. He will have our blessed Lord scourged—not that He is guilty, not that He deserves this penalty, but to satisfy the great, slavering beast that is the mob, and to save his own standing. This compromise will not, of course, placate the mob; a little evil never works a greater good, always spawns a greater evil.

And so the silent Saviour is led away by the rough, bored, sullen soldiers, taken to a musty dungeon chamber, relieved of His outer garments, made to bend over a squat column, and tied by the wrists to it. On His naked back the whips descend, on His arms, His neck, His shoulders, His legs. The scourges are of two kinds: heavy chains ending in iron balls, and thongs of leather toughened in brine and tipped with jagged pieces of bone.

They tear away ribbons of skin, bite into the flesh, macerate nerves and veins, bare the ribs. The person condemned to scourging—under which many men have died—is fair game for the loutish troops. Scourging is for slaves, for those of inferior breed. The very fact that it is ordered for Christ is a sure sign that He is not a Roman citizen, but a mere provincial, a nonentity, perhaps of servile status, hence without rights or recourse, no matter what the soldiers do to Him.

So they zestfully have at the defenseless victim, applying the whips mercilessly, taking out on Him their resentment of His people, who treat them with such cool disdain, vying with one another in feats of brutality, striking the harder as the blood lust rises and they are ravished by that cruelty with which twisted human nature responds to helplessness and, especially, meekness.

Though the Saviour never cries out, He shudders and reels under the ever fiercer deluge of blows. Pain races through His body like a prairie fire. His blood spouts in dozens of scarlet fountains, and His bowed face shines with tears. His beauty is rent to shreds, and in its stead is raw and nauseous ugliness. The strength of His prime of life is smashed, and liquid weakness drowns Him. Pain has obliterated the comeliness of the fairest of the sons of men.

We spell this out in order to study the scourging and thus better understand certain things found in our own times and our own lives.

What in our own times instantly reminds us of the scourging? It is the treatment of their victims by the secret police of the totalitarian dictatorships, whether Nazi or Soviet or of any other sort. Many and many a poor inoffensive Pole or Hungarian or Slovak or Ukrainian or Jew or Chinese has been led into a dungeon, even as was Christ, and there hideously beaten, even as was He. Pilate's palace no longer occupies merely a street corner in Jerusalem; its walls have been widened to take in half the world; its filthy cellars are a subterranean network honeycombing whole continents; and in them unnumbered blameless people have been pummeled to a stinking jelly.

Nor is that all. There are the concentration camps and the slave labor camps with their profusion of paraphernalia nicely calculated to inflict the ultimate in pain on the helpless, to make them suffer vehemently and perish ignominiously. There are the gas chambers, the crematoria, the machinery for turning human beings into fertilizer and soap. The scourges wielded on Christ are today wielded more generally and more viciously than ever before in human history.

And this has led some observers, considering the extent of the horrible spectacle, to say: "God is dead, swallowed up without trace in the salt sea of abominations." But these people have got it just the wrong way round. God is not discredited. God has not done this thing; He is no barbarous, bloodthirsty monster. Men have done it, and precisely those men who begin with the assumption that God is dead and, faultless in their logic, conclude that, if God is dead, then nothing prevents —indeed, everything prompts—the outraging of men, the violation and the stamping out of the human dignity which has but one root and one reason: namely, that man is the image of God.

We have not yet seen anything of the sort in our

hemisphere, because Christianity here still retains, openly or unguessed at, some of its influence over the concepts and the conduct of men. But the steady decline among us of the force of the idea of God means that it is surely coming here as already it has come elsewhere.

We should note well that Christ is brought to the pillar of flagellation by the co-operation of two forces which loathe each other and would like to destroy each other, but nonetheless can act together against God: a pagan empire which does not know the true God, and a far from pagan nation which, knowing the true God, has chosen to disregard His will and to reject His representative. There is an awful warning for our generation in this. The treatment given the Saviour in the place of scourging epitomizes what is always done to man when God is ruled out or overruled in human councils.

Narrowing the horizon and dipping into our own lives and those of our dear ones, what do we discover which links up with this episode in the Passion of our blessed Lord? Pain. It takes little searching to find pain of one sort or another in any life; it takes little reflection to establish a connection between it and what Christ endured.

Pain is a condition of living almost as much as is breathing. No life is free of it. The infant feels its jagged tooth, the aged person feels its flailing fist, and so does everyone else between these extremes of our journey. We dislike it; we strive to evade it; we do everything possible to allay and end it. It is an evil, and we want no part of it. It is an indignity, too, plainly proving our vulnerability, our liability to disease, injury, dissolution, showing us that, despite our swollen pride of life, we amount to very little after all.

But is pain a total loss? In many lives, yes; in them it is simply an inexplicable and unmitigated disaster which at all costs is to be avoided or, if it comes despite the most elaborate precautions, is to be met with the ice of stolidity or the flame of rage. But this is not the case with the genuine Christian. For he knows the wonderful thing that Christ has done with pain. Before the scourging one might understandably consider pain a sterile curse; but not after the scourging, because there at the bloodied pillar Christ gave us a lesson in the use, and indeed the usefulness, of pain.

He used it as a means of making satisfaction to His Father for the sins of our race, for gaining us pardon and restoration to the divine friendship. Offense grievous past measuring had been given the eternal Majesty by our sins, and it could be offset only by a sacrifice proportionate to the harm done. Sacrifice requires a victim—here the Son of God become man. It requires the destruction of the victim—here begun in the scourging. By an act of the will, Christ embraced pain and turned it into sacrifice which would remove God's aversion to us and renew the flow of God's grace into our arid souls.

Realizing this, we must not waste the pain which comes to us. We must not just put up with it stoically, or angrily shout maledictions. Rather, we must see it as a precious opportunity to join directly in our blessed Lord's Passion, to share in His ordeal and its merits, to fill up (as St. Paul puts it) what is wanting of the sufferings of Christ. Here is one of the most powerful means for growth in Christlikeness, and the tragedy is that most of us never even recognize that fact, much less do anything about it, when the scourges of pain are laid upon us.

Instead, we are preoccupied with questions concerning the responsibility for the pain we feel or witness. The sufferer from the wanton plunderer that is cancer passionately inquires: "What have I ever done that God makes or lets this happen to me?" The survivors of the sturdy, clean-limbed, clean-hearted, richly promising young man who is suddenly immobilized, then dispatched, by paralysis ask: "Why did God decree or permit the wasting of this strength and potentiality for good?" The weeping mother of the bonny babe wrenched and smothered by furious convulsions says: "How could a good God allow the sinless little thing to agonize and die in this horrible way?"

There is one answer to all such questions, and it is this: Did Christ deserve to suffer and to die? What had He done to earn the chastisement of the lash? What debt had He incurred that called for this cruel requital? You will hunt in vain for fault in Him. He is utterly, snowily innocent. But, through His Incarnation, He has become a member of our race and heir to its sorrows and its stripes. This is the lot of man on earth since original sin—to suffer.

Seeing Him torn by the whips, we get a graphic lesson in a strange truth about mankind, a truth at once terrible and magnificent: namely, the solidarity of the human species. We are all a single family, a single body, and cannot be divorced one from another, regardless of the differences of race or period or social status or wealth or whatever. We are members one of another.

We suffer because of one another. This is obvious in the sense that someone's mistake leads to a crash and a holocaust in which fifty plane passengers anguish and perish, or someone else's wickedness precipitates the maiming and slaughter of millions in war. It is not so obvious, but quite as true, in the sense that whatever pain comes to us stems from Adam's sin and the sins of his descendants. Christ's pain stems from the soldiers, from Pilate, from the mob, yes; but also from Adam, from every man, from you, from me. To see our own pains traced down to their roots will be one of the amazing experiences of the general judgment; we shall then know how literally true it is that on earth we are one inseparable, interconnected, interacting body.

We shall also be amazed to see our pains traced up to their flowering in the lives of others. For if we suffer because of one another, we also can suffer *for* one another. Pain can be a means of our bearing one another's burdens. Just as Christ had no responsibility for the guilt He expiated through suffering willingly accepted, so we may have no responsibility for the guilt which we get the opportunity to expiate through suffering willingly accepted. The cancer victim's resignation may be the price of salvation for a person he has never heard of, in a remote land, speaking an alien tongue. The rosy youth's unprotesting death may mean life everlasting for a sinner old in years and in evil. The obliteration of the mortal spark in a baby, though the baby cannot consciously agree to suffering, still may lead to reform and lead on to fervor in some bystander. We bring pain on to one another; we can bring one another on to heaven by our pain.

Pain, then, proves our unity one with another.

Pain taken as Christ took it can prove the instrument for welding us in everlasting unity with His Father who is also our Father. Here is the astounding revelation of the dingy dungeon, the mystery of the scourging unriddled.

4

HUMILIATION

The scourging was ordered by the governor. The crowning with thorns which followed it was something the soldiers devised and did on their own. It was then the custom to let the executioners have some sport with their victim before finishing him off. They might do what they liked with him to entertain themselves and any onlookers.

In this case, the soldiers seize on Christ's words to Pilate, "I am a king," as the theme of their mockery. There is special relish in it for them, because they are Samaritans and Greeks from Syria and therefore fiercely hostile to the Jews. They will in ironical earnest show these people what a king of the Jews looks like and how he should be treated.

Weakened, dizzied, His body ploughed and planked with pain, Christ is thrust upon a paint-less, uneven-legged stool, which shall serve as His throne. The brilliance of this inspiration sends the soldiers into gales of glee. A tattered cloak, once a gorgeous scarlet, now weathered to insipidity and threadbare, shall be a robe of state. It is flung around Christ's shoulders.

For a crown, what? How about some of those pieces of thorn bush, piled in a corner for use in kindling a fire to take the cutting edge off morning or evening? Weave them together, and then put the bristling circlet upon His head. Men turn all the lower orders of creation against the Creator: the animal, in the leather thongs of the scourges; the vegetable, in the branches of thorn bush; the mineral, in the nails soon to be used for the crucifixion. Lord of all, is He? All shall have a raucous voice in the denial of that claim and in punishing Him for its impudence.

Have a care, the crown is slipping off. It will never do to have a king lose His crown or wear it awry. Keep the thing on Him. Lay the flat of your swords across it, and press down, press down with all the weight of your beefy bodies, so that this rustic pretender may be fully aware that He is crowned. Do the long, tough, needle-pointed thorns draw blood? So much the better, for now His brow and His cheeks match the rest of Him in the deep dye of royal red.

And here on the floor—what happy fortune!—is a reed. Stick it between His still bound, twitching hands for a sceptre. Now we have a king indeed.

A king of fools, a king of mountebanks, a king of outcasts, a king of vermin, a king of the witless, the luckless, the helpless, the dregs and the scum, a king of the dead and decayed.

How shall He be reverenced? Why, with blows of the fists, blows of the open hand, with streams of spittle and torrents of taunts, with derisive genuflection and grimace, with roaring, reverberant, gasping laughter.

There are two thoughts to take away from this appalling scene.

First, we are aghast at what these soldiers are doing. The enormity of it leaves us speechless, sends our hearts plummeting. Yet His tormentors know Jesus Christ only as a carpenter from some inconsequential village in the north, who has gone about stirring up the people and making fantastic claims, hence has rendered Himself both ridiculous and dangerous. Obviously, to them He is a simpleton, but at the same time a sinister sort of simpleton. To knock some sense into Him and to pay Him out for His swindling and rousing of the rabble is only fit and proper.

See Christ with the soldiers' eyes and there will come home to you the full impact of those words of St. Paul: that Christ, "though He was by nature God, did not consider being equal to God a thing to be clung to, but emptied Himself, taking the nature of a slave and being made like unto

47

men. And appearing in the form of man, He hum-
bled Himself, becoming obedient to death, even to
the death of the cross." We see Christ with a sun-
burst halo, which sets Him off unmistakably from
all others. The soldiers saw no tracery of light
about His head; they saw only a lacklustre slave.

If a very small child breaks to bits a goblet of
priceless Venetian glass, we cannot charge him
with the fullness of the fault. He knew he was
destroying something, and that to do so was wrong,
and to this extent he can be held guilty. But he
knew nothing of the market value of what he
broke, and he cannot, then, be taxed with responsibility for all of the objective havoc he has perpe-
trated. Something of the sort is true of the soldiers.
They knew that they were outraging a fellow human being, and, in the measure that they did so,
they are answerable for the deed. They did not
know that they were outraging the Second Person
of the Trinity, for He had come to them in the
form of a slave; therefore, conscious and deliberate atrocity upon the Godhead is not to be laid to
them.

Accordingly, our indignation should in the main
be reserved for ourselves. We are in worse case
than the soldiers. We know, where they did not;
we know what they did not. The identity of Jesus
Christ has been clear to us for years and years;
from earliest youth, in most instances. Were we

not, when but a toddling two or three, trained to bow our heads at mention of that Name, to regard that Name as above all others, and the One who bears it as above all others? Yes, we know, have long known. Yet are we, in fact, better than the soldiers in our treatment of Christ?

We crown Him with thorns more than once, perhaps habitually. Every time we choose someone else, something else, over Him, we crown Him with thorns. When we elect the sins of the flesh, we crown Him with thorns. When we prefer money to Him, we crown Him with thorns. When we conceal or compromise our religion in the hope of getting business or social or political advantage, we crown Him with thorns. When we start our children on a path which may possibly give them a chance at worldly gain, and will certainly put them in danger of the loss of their faith and, eventually, their souls, we crown Him with thorns. When we do injustices to others (in speech, over a cup of tea, for example), and when we breach the supreme law of charity, we crown Him with thorns. In all such circumstances we say to Him, in effect: "With me, You are entirely secondary; You count for nothing. I set You at naught. I make light of You, make sport of You. I belittle You, buffet You, laugh You to scorn and set others to doing the same."

Secondly, this scene should spur us to consider

vidual in it should think us less than splendid specimens. Hence, a great deal of our energy goes into scheming and contriving to enhance our reputation. So much so that we have little time left for scrutinizing and improving our spiritual life. If others, viewing the surface phenomena of our lives, think well of us, then what does it matter if God, piercing to the depths of our being, to the rude reality of us, thinks ill of us?

Christ, under the tempest of ruffianly abuse, is sustained by one thought—that His Father understands, though no one on earth, except His Mother, does. Everyone else sees a clownish figure, a rustic spieler who has been shown up as a fraud and is being reduced to a gory pulp, to the vociferous amusement of the whole palace cohort. But His Father sees a will set steadfastly on redemptive sacrifice, no matter what may be thought and done by others. We occasionally say in criticism of someone: "He will stoop to anything," meaning that this person has the brass to resort to extremes of crassness or crookedness in order to get money or power for himself. In a very different sense, we can say of the striated and thorn-crowned Christ: "He will stoop to anything," meaning that He will endure every sort and degree of humiliation in order to get grace and glory for us.

From this incident we must learn three things. First, we must learn to put at its true value the fallible opinion of the world. The world's misjudgment of Christ is an overpowering and unanswerable demonstration of the feebleness, and, indeed, the nonsensicality, of the world's way of estimating worth and pigeon-holing people. If it was so wrong about Him, how can it be right about anyone else? We have spoken already of the astounding surprises in store at the general judgment. Here is another—the discovery of who, in life and eternity, is really important—the famous, influential, licentious millionaire who walks the office floors by day, or the insignificant, devout colored woman who scrubs those same floors by night.

Secondly, we must learn always to judge according to the divine standard, and not the worldly. That is, in making up our minds about the whole course of our lives or some particular point in them, to have our decision determined by spiritual factors, theological principles, moral values. The balance should be swung not by what the neighbors might think, but by what God surely thinks. Also, in our rating and treatment of others, we must look not to glamor and glibness, to wardrobe and wealth, to prominence and popularity, but to virtue which so often is hidden behind a commonplace or even ridiculous facade.

Lastly, we must learn to find in humiliation not an intolerable ill, an insupportable sorrow, but a mighty means of doing penance for ourselves and others, of growing in holiness, of becoming one with Him, who, when He was disdained and insulted, jibed at and jabbed at, slapped and spit upon, uttered no syllable of protest, since He realized that, as St. Paul expresses it, "The foolish things of the world has God chosen to put to shame the 'wise,' and the weak things of the world has God chosen to put to shame the strong, and the base things of the world and the despised has God chosen, and the things that are not, to bring to naught the things that are; lest any flesh should pride itself before Him."

5

CONDEMNED

"Jesus is condemned to death." Try to imagine that you are hearing these words for the first time. Like contact with a charged electric wire, they produce a shock. "Jesus is condemned to death." Can it be that the Son of God, He who is Maker and Master and Measure of all creation, is, by one of His own creatures, doomed to die? Outrageous? Preposterous? It is true, literally true.

Moreover, it is not wholly unexpected. We should have been prepared for it by our reading of the Gospel. For this is not the first time that He has been sentenced to death.

There was, for example, the edict of Herod that all male children of two years or under, in or about Bethlehem, should be butchered. Its object was the death of Jesus when He was still but a tiny child. The egomaniac king would suffer no rival in his realm, hence would snuff out the life of one to whom the ancient prophecies pointed.

Hardly had the incarnate Saviour begun His mortal life than His instant death was ordered. He escaped only because Mary and Joseph snatched Him away into Egypt.

Again, in His manhood, during His public ministry, the people of His own town, Nazareth— not a mad monarch, but His old neighbors— sought to kill Him. One morning in the synagogue He had read aloud to them the words of the prophet Isaias: "The Spirit of the Lord is upon me. He has anointed me and sent me out to preach the gospel to the poor, to restore the broken-hearted, to bid the prisoners go free and the blind to receive their sight, to set the oppressed at liberty, to proclaim a year when men may find acceptance with the Lord." He put down the scroll. He looked for a long moment at the people. Then, calmly, He said: "This Scripture which I have read in your hearing is today fulfilled." There was a stunned silence, while their minds grappled with the claim He was making— that of being the Messias. Then they "rose up and thrust Him out of the city and took Him up to the brow of the hill on which their city was built, to throw Him over it." They would have killed Him, but He "passed through the midst of them and went on his way."

Still again, in Jerusalem, during the great Feast of the Tabernacles, He preached to the throng in the Temple. He reproached them for the sterile formalism of their religion and more than hinted at His own divinity and the tremendous change He would effect in men's relationship with God. They murmured. They grumbled. Instead of acknowledging His divinity, they flung it in His teeth that He was possessed of a devil. They took up stones to hurl at Him and batter Him to death. "But," says the Gospel, "Jesus hid Himself and went out of the Temple."

Much could be said of various other threats on our blessed Lord's life, the impulses to violence against Him, the plots and schemes of scribes and Pharisees and chief priests to arrest and dispatch Him. All of these came to nothing, but only, as St. John remarks more than once, because the Saviour's time to die had not yet come.

But come it would. Did He not predict as much, again and again, in ever-plainer words, to the scandal of the Apostles? And come it did. Pilate speaks the words. The Saviour is led away. In a few hours, He the Giver and Sustainer of life, will be dead. The life of Christ is, from the outset, closely overshadowed with the threat of death, overhung with the sentence of death, and finally the threat is fulfilled, the sentence carried out. This has, for the Christian, more meanings than may be obvious.

In the first place, it tells us something of the

history of the Church. At the Last Supper, Christ had warned the Apostles that what was about to be done to Him would be done, in turn, to His followers. "In the world, you will find only tribulation . . . They will persecute you just as they have persecuted me . . . The time is coming when anyone who puts you to death will claim that he is performing an act of worship to God." His words were, of course, proved true. Each of the Apostles was harshly used by the world, suffering much because of his preaching of the Gospel, and every one of them except St. John died a martyr's death. So it was to be with literally millions of others of the Saviour's followers in subsequent centuries.

There were the martyrs of Jerusalem and those of imperial Rome, not merely in the city itself, but wherever, about the Mediterranean, the Roman eagle unfurled its brassy wings. In age after age, in country after country, the company of those sentenced to death for Christ has been swelled. It is not a mere matter of myriad individual deaths. It is a matter of Christ's Mystical Body's being continuously, like Him, sent to death. How often it has heard the same sentence. In Spain under the Moors, in the England of the first Elizabeth, in Ireland under Cromwell, in France at the time of the Revolution, in the Japan of the samurais, on this continent as the Iroquois murdered and pillaged, in Nazi Germany, in Lithuania, Latvia, Estonia, Poland, Hungary, Yugoslavia, Czechoslovakia, China, as the Communist grip closed upon each. Always and ever the same decree: "To the cross, to death." Christ's words have been ceaselessly borne out. We must realize, then, that this is the way it is meant to be, that this is what the Church to which we belong can look for from the world—the sentence of death.

Perhaps we will never have to endure anything of the sort; in these days no one can be sure. But certainly in some sense, we share in the sentence of death passed on Christ and all who are Christ's. How?

Consider what St. Paul says in his first epistle to the Christians of Corinth. "It seems as if God had destined us," he writes, "to be in the lowest place of all, like men under sentence of death . . . We are fools for Christ's sake . . . We are despised . . . We are the world's refuse; everyone thinks himself well rid of us."

Strong words, surely. Perhaps exaggerated? No. The genuine Christian, the Christian who truly and fully lives his religion, is indeed, in the world's eyes, foolish, weak, despicable, so much refuse. The world sentences him to death, not necessarily physical death, but the death of nonentity, of

not counting, of not belonging, of being ignored
as insignificant. This is demonstrably true, perhaps
from our own experience.

The faith of the Christian, for example, is com-
monly held to be superstition: a pack of fantastic
and crippling nonsense. His concern with God and
the soul and grace and sin is regarded as preoccu-
pation with empty fictions. His prayer is con-
sidered a witless exercise in talking to himself or
to the vacant air. His assistance at Mass is looked
upon as unintelligent participation in mumbo-
jumbo absurd except among primitive peoples.
His abstaining from meat on Fridays is thought
to be something irrational and fear-induced, like
not stepping on sidewalk cracks. And so forth. To
be a Catholic means, in a certain measure, sometimes greater and sometimes lesser, to have the
world pass on us a sentence of death, cutting us
off from the ranks of those who are reasonable and
realistic, who are alert, knowledgeable, progres-
sive, sophisticated.

It often means, too, a sentence of death upon
our ambitions. We cannot obtain a certain position
in business or government, we cannot enter a certain stratum of society, we cannot achieve a certain standing in a profession, because we are
Christ's and that means that we cannot totally
conform to the world's views and standards. We
are penalized because we have convictions and

commitments which we will not alter or accommodate at the world's wish. Gifts, potentialities, aspirations which we possess will be to some degree frustrated, aborted, because the world demands, in exchange for success, compromises which are a betrayal of Christ.

Is this not hard on the Christian, perhaps too hard? Are we not asked to give up too much, forego too much, for the sake of fidelity to Christ? There steals upon us the temptation to accede, at least somewhat, to the wisdom of the world, instead of adhering to what St. Paul calls God's foolishness. Or we nurse a feeling of resentment. Christ, before Pilate, did neither. He did not waver. Nor did He whine. He stood fast. He uncomplainingly accepted the sentence. Capitulation was unthinkable, for the world's terms are always unconditional surrender. Unthinkable, too, was rancor, for, as He was shortly to say: "they know not what they do."

But *we* know what we do. Or do we? Do we know that, long before the world passes sentence of death on us, another sentence of death has already been executed upon us? It is an idea which we find St. Paul constantly repeating. He says, for example: "We who were taken up into Christ's baptism, have been taken up, all of us, into His death . . . In our baptism we have been buried with Him, died with Him." What does this mean? Hasn't it a ring of incongruity—"in our baptism, we have been buried with Him, died with Him?" Haven't we always thought of baptism, which made us Christians, as a life-giving sacrament, as effecting our birth into the life of grace? And here is St. Paul speaking of baptism as taking us up into *death,* not life.

There is no contradiction here. St. Paul means that, once baptized, once become Christians, we are dead to sin. "Our former nature has been crucified with Him and the living power of guilt annihilated, so that we are the slaves of guilt no longer." The person just baptized, infant or adult, is free of original sin, actual sin. Sin, which formerly proliferated in him like weeds, now has no place in him. The ideal is that, dead to sin, he should not sin again. He should be dead to what induces to sin. We speak of being "dead to the world." As slang it means being fast asleep. But literally it means something quite wonderful— being fast asleep to the world's allurements to evil, and wide awake to God. "You are dead, and your life is hid with Christ in God." The Christian should no longer live on the merely natural level, the level of the fallen world, the corrupt flesh, where the devil holds sway and sows ruin. Rather, he should live wholly, exclusively, on the supernatural level, the level of grace, possessed and directed in all that he does and all that he is by divine charity, by the Godhead dwelling within him. He is dead to existence as an isolated, corrupt, unredeemed individual, and has begun to live as a member of Christ, incorporated into His Mystical Body, on a plane and in an atmosphere far above those of the world which knows neither God nor His Son.

The world sees in Christ being sentenced to death by Pilate only a failure and a fool. The Christian, too, it sees only as a failure and a fool, who inexplicably cuts himself off from self-indulgence, distractions, absorption in material goods, who fasts and abstains, gets up early on bitter winter mornings to go off to church, restricts the sexual act to marriage, limits his drinking, denies himself luxuries to give to the needy, avoids reading matter and entertainment which are pagan in spirit, and so forth. The world does not see that Christ crucified conquers death. No more does it see that the Christian crucified is vibrantly alive with faith, hope, love, with the presence of God, with the beginnings of eternal glory. Christ dies that we may live more abundantly; we die that we may live more abundantly. "With Christ I am nailed to the cross. And I live, now not I, but Christ lives in me."

6

PATIENCE

Go now with Christ upon the road to Calvary. Pilate has shown Him, lurid from the lashes and wearing a blood-jewelled crown, to the multitude, in the hope that the pitiable figure might melt the stones that had replaced hearts in their breasts and eyes in their heads. But the only crying they do is with lungs and throat and tongue. Shouts of "Crucify him!" fly up like a skyful of vultures. And Pilate does their bidding. He sentences our blessed Lord to the cross, has a placard inscribed "Jesus of Nazareth, King of the Jews" hung about His neck, and starts Him on a journey, the end of which nobody present suspects.

The cross is crushing for one so debilitated as the poor Man from Nazareth. He has to carry it through the streets, through one of the gates, across the moat, out to a little rise of earth beyond the city walls. His myriad wounds nag at Him, the burning sun nags at Him, the stones of the pavement nag at Him. But the torment inflicted by these is as nothing to that inflicted by the mob.

From near and far pilgrims have come to participate in Jerusalem's observance of the Pasch. Many present are from beyond the borders of Palestine, even from beyond the sea. Many more are from various parts of the Holy Land: from Capharnaum, Nazareth, Naim, Jericho, Bethany, Bethlehem, from towns along the Jordan and hamlets dotting the shores of the Sea of Galilee.

There is reason to suppose that every phase of the life of Christ is represented in the throng: people who were in Bethlehem when He was born, people from Nazareth where He spent three decades, people from places where He preached, others from places where He wrought miracles, perhaps beneficiaries of His power to heal, certainly beneficiaries of His power to stir the soul to life. All His mortal years are there for Him to read and review as He searches the faces of people who have seen Him before, under very different circumstances. And with but miserably few exceptions, they were now hostile, indifferent, or prevented by fear from letting any glimmer of recognition or concern show in their looks.

The throng filled the narrow streets, jostling the Saviour and retarding Him at every step. He was like a spent swimmer trying to make headway against a furious sea. Imprecations were screamed at Him; the garbage of vituperation was flung at Him; He was reviled and ridiculed. All the pent-up hatreds and resentments, all the secret frustration and shame of hundreds of people who, under everyday conditions, appeared to be simple, straight-forward folk with no dark and dirty corners in their being, were taken out on Him in such a paroxysm of inhumanity as characterizes a lynch mob. The unchaste, the impious, the money-worshipers, the offenders against family loyalty, the ingrates, the betrayers of friendship, the back-biters, the habitual liars, the cheaters, those sick with envy, the anger-wasted, the gluttons, the disappointed, all spewed upon Him the filth rotting in the hidden recesses of their being. They showed forth the truth that here indeed was not just a man laden with a cross, but the Lamb of God laden with, and taking away, the sins of the world. This is the sight that we should see at the *Agnus Dei* of the Mass.

Soon He is gone and the streets grow less choked, and the bellows of the hawkers of various wares resume, and the tinkle of camel bells is again heard, and pannier-carrying donkeys can move along under their owners' prodding, and people fall to talking once more of the small things of familiar routine, and the brief excitement kindled by the passing of three condemned men dies out.

It was not a very long journey, that made by Christ. It could be covered in fifteen or twenty minutes by a person in normal health, in normal circumstances. But our blessed Lord was not in normal health; He was a strident clamor of wounds. And the circumstances were not normal; the streets were coagulated with wrought up men and women. Even so, the trip from Pilate's palace to Golgotha could hardly have taken more than an hour. To the Victim, of course, that hour might well have seemed a leadenly lagging year.

Does it not seem to us, as in our turn we go whatever unsought and sometimes surprising way of the cross is appointed for us, that the path of pain is interminable? Do we not find it like one of those situations in a dream, in which, as we struggle to move forward, the ground underfoot is like molten tar and the very air an impenetrable net?

Consider the person who has a long, wasting illness. He knows that he is doomed. Palliatives can give him a little temporary relief like a vagrant breeze on a sultry summer day, but the ravages of the disease go implacably on. Day and night he suffers, his life draining away drop by dallying drop, each drop with its sting of acid. Will there never be a stop to the process? Will the jaws of the vise in which he is being squeezed never come together? Is the possibility of final release just an illusion? I wonder if you have ever heard a person, whose body is being gradually ruined by an ailment, desperately pray that he may soon die? It happens. His way of the cross appears endless to him.

Or consider the mother on tenterhooks over the health of a child. Something certainly is wrong, but what is it? The doctors make their examination, and confess to bafflement. It could be one thing, it could be another. It could be something grave or fatal, or it could be only a relatively minor disturbance. Time alone will tell; more symptoms will have to manifest themselves in their unhurriable season, or tests which require a considerable while for the yielding of answers will have to be undergone. The mother feels that she is being flayed alive, inch by inch of her skin being torn away, while she awaits the unveiling of the truth.

Then there is the person in search of a job. He has no kindred to supply or help him with the very essentials of existence. He is not so young any more: one of those people in their fifties (sometimes even in their forties) whom employers are reluctant to take on, except in the most pressing emergency. Perhaps his health is not of the best. Perhaps he requires certain rather expensive medicines for heart trouble or diabetes. Little by little his small savings are leaking away. And still nothing turns up. There is this lead, that half-promise, a flurry of "if's," but nothing materializes. How long will it be until something does?

Again, there is the person fighting a perpetual battle with a sin or a temptation. A woman, for example, who is forever having to accuse herself of sins of uncharity. She has a habit of making slighting remarks either to people or about people. After each lapse she has a feeling of self-disgust, a feeling as of having soiled herself. She resolves not to do this thing again. But she does, probably very soon. Again the feeling of nastiness, of a foul taste in the mouth. She tells the sorry story in confession, resolves that a new page is here and now being turned. But the next confession is much like the last. Will she ever be other than this? Discouragement sets in, the inclination to give up the effort to eliminate a vice and build a virtue.

As for temptation, that to impurity is probably as common as any. We are all of the earth earthly, of the flesh fleshly. We are, by definition, rational animals, not the same as beasts surely, but having much in common with beasts, including the sexual appetite. It is sharp, persistent, insatiable, by no means evil in itself, but all too ready to get out of bounds and seize and make shipwreck of the human person. It will be with us all our days, ready to override our will whenever it detects weakness, wavering there. And it is fed constantly by the senses—by what we see, what we hear, what we touch. The imagination stores away sensual images, like rolls of film or phonograph records, and plays them over and over. We are beset with vivid and attractive solicitation of our consent to impure thoughts, impure actions. We are constantly so beset. Sometimes we think we simply cannot go on resisting, since the trial is so protracted. Dismiss the temptation and it comes back again and again and again, like insects battering at a screen hour after hour. We come to believe that we cannot win, that we are obsessed, that we shall go mad.

All such experiences are related to that of Christ upon the way of sorrows. They cannot be understood or used aright unless the relationship is recognized. If they do not have plainly in the background One who labors along the streets of Jerusalem on a day in spring, they can be a total loss. They are endurable and profitable only if that background is there and in focus.

Christ here teaches us two things: patience and perseverance. In this era of restlessness, we need instruction in patience. Our problems, as persons and as a community, are many and serious. We want them solved instantly and finally. A war, hot or cold, which grinds on for months and years without end irritates us; either let there be a quick decision or we will switch our attention from it.

Effective co-operation among the nations to remove the roots of misunderstanding and distress must be effected with a stroke of the pen or we turn our backs. A deep and ancient fissure in the social body of the nation must be closed immediately and without scar or we will throw up our hands. Capital and labor must settle their differences once for all or we will say: "A plague o' both your houses." Any sort of annoying situation in which we are involved (be it a chronic stomach condition or an unpleasant association at the office or having to live with querulous in-laws) must be cleared up immediately or we seethe and sputter. Be patient, Christ tells us as He goes so slowly to Calvary; bear your cross as I do mine.

He also tells us to persevere. Does it seem that, under trial, we can hold out no longer, that we must have relief or we shall collapse or explode? Watch Him going steadily ahead, taking one torturing step after another. He falls? Yes, but He always gets up and continues on the way. He does not round on the crowd in rage; He does not shake a fist at the seemingly unconcerned heavens and say to His Father: "I have had enough; I quit." No, He keeps at the tedious and tormenting task set Him. And so must we.

7

FAILURE

Christ fell three times on the way to Calvary. Some artists have distinguished the falls one from another by representing Christ in the first as falling to His knees, in the second as falling upon hands and knees, in the third as falling full-length. There is reason for such differentiation, for, surely, as the Saviour went farther forward through the dense crowd, through the humid, fetid streets, He grew ever weaker and wearier and came closer to total collapse.

There is, however, another sort of differentiation to be noted. The falls of Christ, like His agony, are symbolic as well as physical. They signify trials of the spirit as well as of the flesh.

The journey to Calvary takes place only a few days after Palm Sunday, when many in Jerusalem hurried out beyond the city walls to shout their greetings to our blessed Lord, to throw their cloaks down as carpeting for His path, to wave palm branches, and to cry out: "Blessed is he who comes in the name of the Lord, blessed is the king of Israel." Thus they acknowledged His ascendancy over them, the reverent regard in which they held Him, the great things they expected of Him. Perhaps the jubilant procession came through this very street where now He falters under the ponderous cross and falls for the first time.

Such a coincidence would have a particular point, for this first fall typifies His fall in popular estimation. How warmly, how unreservedly, the people had hailed Him as He preached to them, worked His miracles, set at naught those who would trap Him. "No man has spoken as this man speaks," they had delightedly said to one another, When He freed a man of palsy, "they were filled with awe at seeing it, and praised God for giving such powers to men." When He gave sight to two blind men, and speech to one who was dumb, the onlookers murmured: "Nothing like this was ever seen in Israel." At His bidding the lame walked, the lepers were cleansed, the dead rose to life, and the people, beholding, were astonished, and they deeply venerated Him. When He stilled winds and waves, the crew of the vessel in which He was crossing the waters fell trembling at His feet and spoke of Him as the Son of God. When He fed hungry thousands with a few loaves and fishes, they sought to make Him their king, and He had to slip away to thwart this scheme. "Look," said the thoroughly vexed Pharisees, "the whole world has turned aside to follow him."

He had, then, known unexampled popularity. He had evoked a response, gained a respect which no man of His time could match. His wonders were on every tongue, and almost every tongue sounded His praise. The chorus of applause had come to a deafening pitch only five days before.

And now? Now there is not a whisper of the acclamation with which lately the hills had rung, and the city's cobblestones. Now not a word to His credit is spoken. Now not the slightest gesture of recognition is made. His heart-kindling discourses, His marvels of healing, reversing death, commanding the forces of nature, were as if they had never been. The multitude, the *same* multitude, saw in Him now only a fraud bereft of His powers of demagoguery and deception, drowned in disgrace, helpless against governor, high priest, soldiery, against whip, thorn, gibbet. How He had declined in their esteem! This is the first fall—the fall from mastery of the world's respect to the mire of disrepute.

There is a second fall. Christ had fired men's minds with a vision of human transformation after the wintry centuries of sin's dominance. He had pictured for them a splendid new order. In it, justice would prevail, love would reign, peace would be untroubled. The poor in spirit would come into their own. The patient would inherit the earth. Those who mourned would be comforted, to weep no more. The hypocrite would be exposed, the proud set down, the ostentatious put to shame, the avaricious denied his treasure, the wicked requited.

The people were moved to exultation at this prospect. But they misunderstood in expecting that the new day would dawn instantly and effortlessly. They were mistaken in believing that a tremendous spiritual revolution would be achieved magically and at once. It was at hand, they believed, as near as tomorrow. And believing this, they were exhilarated by the prospect of humanity changed, wonderfully, drastically changed, in the twinkling of an eye. They yielded themselves to impossible hopes.

But look now at the One whom they understood to have promised a speedy, painless revolution of the spirit. Look at Him on hands and knees, like an animal; His eyes glazed with agony; His head drooping with fatigue; His body quivering with the pain of a hundred lashes; His clothes drenched with sweat, splotched with blood, grotesquely bunched about legs twitching with the effort to rise; the soldiers railing and cursing at Him; the mob jeering Him; the corrupt priests gloating over Him. *He* usher in a kingdom in which wrongs would be righted, the slavery of sin would be broken, men would be reconciled with God, virtue would bloom and fruit, the wounded race would be healed and lifted to a new plane of existence? The very notion of *His* effecting anything of the sort provoked laughter hideous in its scorn. His kingdom would never come! This was a worse fall, far more excruciating for Christ, the collapse of credence not simply in His powers, but also in His mission.

But the third is worse still. It occurred in the very shadow of Calvary. It threw Him flat upon the earth, like a heap of refuse in the roadway, His face against the earth, His arms and legs outflung and motionless. This is the most humiliating, the most desolate of the falls. All His strength has drained away; all His resources are spent: He is abject, abandoned.

Abandoned. What is it that He will shortly be saying from the cross? What is it that He will be hoarsely crying in the intimidating darkness? *"Eloi, Eloi, lamma sabachthani"*—"My God, my God, why hast Thou abandoned me?"

To be repudiated by men, to be deserted by the Apostles, these were pinpricks in comparison with the dreadful dereliction when even His Father seems withdrawn. He had calmly foretold that the multitude would melt away, that His chosen ones would flee from His side. But of this terrible mystery He had given no intimation. Here was the shattering climax of His ordeal—the unbreakable union with His Father under shadow; a bleak feeling of utter aloneness; all lights quenched and ahead nothing but the roaring arctic night.

If the three falls of Christ are linked with three phases of dereliction for Him, they are also linked with three kinds of experience in our own lives.

First, there is our failure to fulfill the promise which our powers once seemed to justify. We were going to make our mark in this world; such is the universal conviction of youth. We had physical prowess, or intellectual gifts, or aptitudes and skills of one kind or another, or a scintillant personality. These would guarantee us a large measure of distinction, would make us stand out from the crowd, would bring us notable rewards.

Somehow it did not work out that way. We were passed by. Others' estimate of us was revised downward. We proved to be a run-of-the-mill specimen, laboring in some menial capacity, one clerk among many, one mechanic among many, one teacher among many, a dime-a-dozen musician or artisan, a rocket that never left the ground. We just didn't get the breaks, we say; fate was capricious; we were born under an unlucky star. We try to put a smiling face on our conspicuous want of success, to feign indifference. But the failure rankles. Especially are we stung by the realization that people look on us as one who fell far short of his promise.

This corresponds to the first fall of Christ.

Secondly, there is our spiritual failure. As children, we read, or had read to us, the lives of the saints. We eagerly drank in the accounts of their heroic holiness. They lived wholly for God; they lived constantly close to God. They conquered temptations; they never committed a mortal sin; despite obstacles, they steadily advanced in merit; their being was irradiated with the love of God, love of all God's children; they possessed their souls in lively, serene awareness of extraordinary virtue. It would be even so with us. We would do as they had done; we would be what they had been. Of this we were sure.

But what has the event proved to be? Of the high holiness of the saints we find no evidence in our lives. Temptation has surrounded us like a blinding blizzard. We have sinned; often, grievously. Our attempts at building virtue seem fitful and unproductive. How dim and intermittent is our charity. Of steady spiritual strength and its consolations, we know nothing. What mediocrities we are, what runts, what duds. And the years are passing, each finding us still fumbling and backtracking. Those glowing childhood dreams are now lifeless ashes. This corresponds to the second fall of Christ.

Thirdly, there is the moment, experienced by most of us once or more than once, when it seems that God has abandoned us. We cannot get in touch with Him. We cannot pray. We numbly exist in a void. There icily comes over us a feeling that we are irrecoverably cut off from God, that He does not care about us, that we are lost in a parched and trackless wasteland. This corresponds to the third fall of Christ, and is incomparably more devastating than the others. It is possible to go on, even when we become fully aware of our failure to make our mark, even when the discouraging realization of our spiritual shabbiness comes home to us. But this! This is like the stopping of the clock, the stopping of the breath, the extinction of the sun.

Christ's falls were for our redemption. They were also for our instruction and comforting.

We are failures? So, in a way, was He. He was regarded with contempt for His failure to make irresistible use of the powers He had once evidenced. He had not made good, so ran the world's judgment; hence, He was ridiculed, dismissed. But He had done good. And that is the test. With God, making good does not matter. Indeed, *our* making good may mean that *His* wishes and purposes are disregarded. But our doing good, making a go of our marriage, supporting our family, caring for a cantankerous relative, bearing an overwhelming burden, always means that His wishes and purposes are fulfilled.

Again, there is our dissatisfaction with our spiritual state. We simply plod along, making no spectacular progress, doing hardly more than keep on the way? Remember that His failure to produce instantaneously the kingdom men had looked for, longed for, led them to despise Him. His method of bringing it about was, contrary to their expectation, to be slow, arduous, not quick, showy. From His second fall we must learn the worth of quiet, unsensational, tenacious perseverance in the spiritual life, of persistence despite reverses and the absence of grand achievement and gratification. Our simply going ahead may, in God's sight, be making us over bit by bit, bringing us inch by inch to the heights.

Still again, we feel forsaken, teeter on the margin of despair. Think of His final fall, the cry from the cross. These are appalling. Yet, even as He fell prostrate, even as He loosed that awful plea, He was within touching distance of victory, far more so than when He was a magnet for the multitudes or when, after days overflowing with miracles, He prayed peacefully on the hushed mountain under the tranquil stars. The greatest trial is prelude to the greatest triumph.

God's ways are not the world's ways. The seed must fall into the ground and die. We must plumb the depths of failure one after another if we would come at last to the shining shore of success which is eternal life.

8

COMPASSION

Christ's Mother figures not at all in the early stages of the Passion as described in the Gospels. She is not at the Last Supper, not in Gethsemane. Perhaps she is one of the throng surging about the high priest's palace, or Pilate's judgment seat. We do not know. It is only when her Son nears Calvary that she comes into view.

There is then an electric moment when He feels a pair of eyes upon Him. There are hundreds staring at Him, of course. But this is different, this is unique—a summons, a greeting, a caress. He halts, raises His head, looks about. His gaze meets the eyes which were the first He ever saw in His infancy, which lovingly watched over His childhood and youth, which followed Him down the path from home when He turned His back on it to begin His mission, which stood out in the multitudes intent upon His preaching. They are the eyes of His Mother.

And what do they see? They see a Son broken in the prime of life: His rugged body beaten; His clothes, all of her making, fouled; His face disfigured with dirt, blood, spittle, tears; His hair dyed with crimson; His head tightly bound with thorns; and on His back the cumbrous tree on which He is soon to die.

Does despondency sweep over her at the sight? Does she faint? Does she cry out in treble protest? Does she rush to Him, to strike down the cross and envelop Him in her cloak and try to lead Him away? No. She does nothing. Or, rather, she does everything which He would have her do. She plumbs His clouding eyes, she unites her will fast with His, she offers afresh the oblation of her heart, she renews her consent to His sacrifice and joins hers to it. And this, for Him, more than offsets the indignity and torment of what others are doing to Him. There is one who understands and agrees, one whose mind and will are in exact accord with His, one whose compassion is fused with His Passion.

It has been ever so. Mary has understood from the start, has accommodated her will to His from the start. When God spoke to her through Gabriel, her immediate response was: "Be it done to me according to thy word." When Simeon had, in the Temple, reached into the future with His fading eyes and plucked out a prophecy: "Behold, this child is destined to bring about the fall of many and the rise of many in Israel; to be a sign which men will refuse to recognize. . . . And thine own soul a sword shall pierce," she grasped the sombre meaning of this, not only with her mind, but also with her will. When, at twelve, the Child temporarily left her and, after being found, said that He must be about His Father's business, she knew that this foreshadowed much more grievous parting and pain, and she did not demur. At Cana it was her bidding which inaugurated the ministry now so mysteriously culminating.

Once, when He was voicing God's word and was interrupted by the news that His Mother awaited Him without, He had pointed at His hearers and said cryptically: "Here is my Mother." And again, as if clarifying this, when a woman in a crowd called out: "Blessed is the womb that bore thee," He had rejoined: "Nay, rather, blessed are those who hear the word of God and keep it." His Mother's sovereign merit was that her heart was in perfect unison with His own.

This meeting on the approach to Golgotha confirms, sums up, her life-long attitude. Little by little, over the years, she has perceived where the commitment of her whole being to Him would lead, what would be its final exaction, and she has never wavered. She does not draw back now. She sustains Him in His purpose, sends Him on to the cross reinforced.

Under that cross she will stand as He inches along the interminable last mile of agony; as the insults grow sharper on the whetstone of cruelty; as His drooping body tears at the implacable nails; as He speaks, at intervals, His telegraphic farewell; as the day prematurely ages, and unnatural twilight veils the rebel earth; as He delivers His soul to His Father, and dies. All the while, she will be erect, composed, bearing the relentless thrusting of the exquisite sword, never repining, always seconding and sharing in His sacrifice by her own.

There are many things which might be said concerning the meaning of this for each of us today. We confine ourselves to two. The first has to do with Mary's power of understanding, the second with her power of intercession.

We have observed that Mary alone, out of all that turbulent concourse, that raging torrent of prejudice and passion, understood what was happening, what her Son was about. Everyone else misunderstood, either wholly like the leaders of the people, or in part like the Apostles. She understood her Son. She understands us. We, too, are her children. On Calvary she became, by Christ's express decree, the Mother of all men. This is no maudlin gesture, with a vague, figurative meaning. It is a plain statement of a literal fact. We are all

Mary's children, each of us near to her, each of us dear to her. She understands us as no one else does.

Throughout life we long to be understood, especially as difficulties abound. Popular songs vulgarize this yearning, but even they witness to a universal truth. We exult when we suppose that we have found someone who sees us whole and aright, who cuts through appearances and seizes upon the obscure essential truth. Each of us is a mystery even to himself and, much more so, to those about him, however close. Each of us is encompassed with solitariness, ringed with barriers of separation. Others brush our lives, invade them to a certain extent, come superficially in touch with the inner self which the great majority of our acquaintances never divine. But, in the main, we are moatedly apart, and we feel this more keenly as the decades pass.

There was one who, in penetrating, intuitive knowledge of us, perhaps surpassed even husband or wife. That was our mother. She, above all others, read our heart. So little of its contents, of its nuances, did she miss. When we were troubled, try though we might to appear carefree, she sensed our unease and the reason for it. She knew what we were hoping for, planning for, even if we said or suggested nothing, or dissimulated. She was acutely aware of our far from patent weaknesses, deficiencies, and tactfully sought to steer us away from indulging them. Our hidden sorrows, disappointments she discovered. The concealed capacity for good in us, the generous impulses, the creditable motives which were not obvious and which others would be amazed to know of, she recognized and encouraged.

All this we took for granted. But there came a day when she left us, and it was only after that that we rightly estimated the insight which had been hers, and what it had meant, that, in seasons green or leafless, she had understood. We learned the full dimensions of our loss and the great loneliness which would thenceforth engulf us.

It was then that we should have begun to realize what Mary's motherhood means and what is its function in our lives. Our natural mother, however subtle or extensive her understanding of us, was of necessity far behind our heavenly Mother in this.

There is absolutely nothing about us that Mary does not know. She sees to the roots of our being. She sees it in its details, in its entirety. There is no door in our heart to which she does not have the key, no recess of the conscious or subconscious which she does not search. This knowledge is shot through with love. It is no dispassionate x-ray, but the partisan, solicitous comprehension of the Mother who understands a divine Son and looks upon us as His brethren. Lay hold upon this, and we will never again succumb to the dreariness, the depression of being unappreciated, uncared for.

When we pray to her, we can begin with the assumption that she knows all about us. We need not explain ourselves, grope for words which will pin down the elusive truth. She is far more aware of it than we, and can show it to us. All we need do is look at her, as did Christ on the way of sorrows, and she will look at us, speaking no audible word any more than she did to Him, but reaching us, lifting us up, sending us rejuvenated on our way, ready to endure the worst which may eventuate and to transform it into sacrifice merged with Christ's, with hers. In her there is for us comfort past counting, strength past taxing, love past bankrupting. We must turn to her as He did, and we shall be sustained by the assurance of being companioned through whatever wilderness awaits us.

Secondly, there are the consequences for us of her incomparable part in the Passion and death of her Son. United with Him in His ordeal, plunged with Him into the expiatory fires, steadfast at His side until His last breath, she wins titles such as no other can claim. Co-Redemptrix of humanity, she is called, and Mediatrix of all graces, and with justice. When the import of her part in the drama of redemption is clear, these titles are inevitable.

As the sinless representative of the sinful race,

as the Immaculate Mother of a fallen family, she suffered with Him, but not for Him. A divine Person, He needed no one to suffer for Him. She did not suffer for herself. In her was no corruption, no offense; so had she been created, so preserved. In her compassion she suffered for us, as Mother of the Mystical Body of which we are members. Hence is she designated Co-Redemptrix.

What Christ wins by the sacrifice which she shares He puts into her hands for distribution. All graces, flowing from the cross, come to us through her, at her behest. She has the right, the power, to do for her earthly children what she will. Since the heavenly treasure is hers to dispose of, we do not do her excessive honor, as some unthinkingly charge. Indeed, we do not honor her nearly enough, given the role God Himself has assigned her. That role is now being more fully spelled out in the theology of the Catholic Church, and its significance will provide arms and armor in our battle with evil, whether individually or as a unit. We do not honor her nearly enough when we think of her simply as the ideal mother, a beautiful lady in pastel shades, all sweetness and softness and sentimentality. She is the woman clothed with the fiery sun, crowned with the blinding stars, treading on the moon. She is the mighty Queen of heaven and earth, honored by Father, Son, and Holy Spirit, deferred to by seraphim and cherubim who existed in glory before the world began, before she began.

And she is as tenderly concerned about us as she was about her Son when neither His power nor hers was recognized. See her like a true mother, anxious and unsparing of self, stepping out of the hidden world into a homely place in our own times: at LaSalette (wearing a peasant's apron), at Lourdes (in a dubiously regarded grotto), at Fatima (in a place of pasturage). She comes to warn us, to stir us up to fidelity and fervor, to fortify us, to lavish blessings on us.

It is as if she had insisted on visiting us in our need, our peril, and God, though displeased with our stubborn adherence to wrong-doing, could not resist her importuning. With each of these visits there are connected dumfounding wonders and favors, to attest not merely the reality of her presence, but also the magnitude of the power she wields in our behalf. She seems to want to remind us, over and over again, that she can do and stands ready to do prodigious things for us. "Ask and you shall receive," said her Son. And so says she. Ask not just for the cure of ailments, the clearing up of temporal problems, but for the fruits of that immolation of her Son to which she joined the immolation of herself: our sanctification, the conversion of the world, the coming of the kingdom of love.

9

SYMPATHY

A fog of antipathy and contempt closed about Christ as He went the way of expiation and as He hung upon the cross. But here and there the fog was penetrated; here and there sympathy shone through to Him, and understanding. We have spoken of His meeting with His Mother and what it meant and did for Him. It was, of course, unique. But there were notable meetings with others: some women of Jerusalem, Veronica, Simon of Cyrene, Dismas.

The anonymous women were brave-hearted folk. They had the courage to dissent from the howling wolf pack, and to evidence their dissent. Christ had been often in Jerusalem, had taught there, held disputations there, worked miracles there, and doubtless there as elsewhere He had visited, eaten with, comforted, the poor in the dingy back alleys. A few women who may have seen Him on such an occasion, came out this day,

their children clinging to their skirts, not to shout
abuse or derision, but to show compassion, grief.
At a certain point in His dread journey He came
upon them, and they wept as they saw His plight
and spoke simple, tear-drowned words of sympathy, regret. They bewailed His anguish, and the
malice and madness of their fellows. They regis-
tered protest and demonstrated that humanity
had not vanished without trace from these hate-
teeming streets. Whatever the risk, they did the
little that they could for Him who to them represented goodness. We hear of them nothing further.

There was one woman who did more. Veronica,
tradition calls her. Who she was we do not know;
what she did we do know. She stepped out of the
throng, stepped up to the Saviour as He lurched
into sight, pressed a clean napkin or towel to His
face. That face was a welter of blood from the
thorn wounds, dirt from the dungeon under
Pilate's palace and the dunged and dusty street
where He had fallen, spittle from the mouths of
those who reviled Him. These Veronica wiped
away, leaving the gaunt, pale, great-eyed, strained
face clear of filth for a little while. We are told
that on that cloth the Saviour's features were
miraculously imprinted. Perhaps this is true. But
the important thing is that Veronica put sympathy
into action. She did not merely feel sympathy; she
did not merely express sympathy; she translated

sympathy into practical terms. She performed a deed of mercy. Of her further history we have no knowledge.

Simon of Cyrene had no intention of doing anything of the sort. He was compelled, against his will, to help carry the cross. He was simply a bystander, not, it is true, out to see and to cheer the ignominious end of the discredited Galilean, but a man caught in the crowd as he tried to make his way home. Suddenly, startlingly, he found himself singled out and told to pick up the cross and bear it, stout, bronzed countryman that he was, since the doomed Man was dizzy with pain and fatigue. "Who, me?" Simon may have said, must have thought, as the unexpected, unwelcome, outrageous summons came. "Why pick on me? What have I done to deserve this? There are other things I must attend to." But protests availed nothing. He was hauled into the roadway, saddled with the cross, shoved forward.

Forward he went, bent under his abominable burden, grumbling at its weight and awkwardness, at the injustice done him. But he experienced a change. The moment of it, the manner of it, are not recorded. But that Simon, the cross-bearer, became a Christian, and his family with him, we know from the Scriptures, and he is included in the calendar of the saints. Somehow he laid hold not merely of the cross, but also of the meaning of the cross, the meaning of the carrying of the cross.

Then there was Dismas. This is the name given the penitent thief. He did not weep for Christ, succor Him on the way, carry His cross. Dismas had to carry his own cross, and was preoccupied with his own predicament, for he was to be executed alongside Christ. He died upon his cross, but not before apprehending something of the meaning of the cross and the death of Christ.

Dismas did not echo the incredulous "Who, me?" of Simon. He was not surprised to find himself under a cross, on a cross. He was a criminal, no petty offender against the law, but the perpetrator of capital crime. When the second of the criminals flanking Christ on Calvary began to upbraid the Saviour, Dismas silenced him. " 'What,' he said, 'hast thou no fear of God, when thou art undergoing the same sentence? And we justly enough; we receive no more than the due reward of our deeds; but this man has done nothing amiss.' " The innocence of Christ he perceived, the goodness overlaid with physical unsightliness and the scum of calumny. Something of the sublime mystery of the central cross he grasped: goodness, more than ordinary goodness, more than human goodness, suffering unspeakably but not unwillingly, suffering for a purpose, a benign purpose, a transcendent purpose, suffering to save such as he.

"Lord," he said, acknowledging Christ's dominion over him, making an act of submission compound of faith and of love, "remember me when thou comest into thy kingdom." To Simon of Cyrene Christ had said nothing. To Veronica He had said nothing. To the women of Jerusalem He had said: "Weep not for me; but weep for yourselves and for your children." But to Dismas He spoke words which we all long to hear addressed to ourselves: "This day thou shalt be with me in paradise."

There they are—the women of Jerusalem, Veronica, Simon, Dismas. What do they have in common? They are all in touch with the suffering Christ, but in different measure. Studying them, we can find something to imitate in each instance.

Consider the women of Jerusalem. They were among the very few to take a truly human attitude to the Son of Man in agony. The overwhelming majority showed themselves callous, case-hardened, when confronted with appalling anguish. Even if they discerned in Christ no more than a fellow mortal, they should have felt pity and solicitude for Him in His trial. Instead, they were flint-hearted. Their only emotion was relish in the terrible spectacle, sadism. Perhaps to the weeping women, Christ's superhuman qualities were hardly clearer than to the rest, but at least the women were filled to overbrimming with sympathy for a man in the toils of death.

What of us? We like to think of ours as an age in which applied science has made fabulous progress in cutting down suffering, and humanitarianism flourishes unprecedentedly. But the fact seems to be that there exists as much suffering now as in any other age, and insensibility to others' suffering is widespread. The dictators have savaged millions of men and women, torturing them in ways gross and shrewd. Total war has inflicted pain on tens of millions. Hospitals, more numerous and capacious than ever, are jammed. Mental ailments harass a greater proportion of the populace than ever. Fear, anxiety, worry keep us in constant ferment. Suffering is still very much with us; in fact, ours is a suffering age which has forgotten the significance and worth of suffering. This is dismayingly evident in our hospitals, dazzling in equipment and techniques, but sometimes devoid of the spiritual atmosphere indispensable to healing.

Are we indifferent so long as we are spared the rack? Does the suffering of others leave us unmoved? Do we lightly say: "That's life" or "That's their hard luck"? Or do we feel genuine concern, intense sympathy? This is the very minimum required if we are to remain human in an era petrifying, icing over with inhumanity. Wherever we see someone suffering we see Christ suffering. Let this be our rule; it is no fiction.

Feeling is something, but it ranks far below doing. Veronica is touched by the suffering of another and acts to ease it. She cannot halt it, reverse it. The journey to the place of death goes grindingly on. But she does what she can. She cleanses the face of the condemned Man, at the same time cheering His stricken heart.

As for us, do we, confronted with suffering, say: "I am very sorry" and let it go at that? Do we feel, without ever translating feeling into concrete assistance? Unless we do what we can in the way of practical help, we are probably mere sentimentalists, dissolving in tears at the thought of another's suffering, yet drawing away, running away if there is any likelihood of our being asked to sit up all night, look after the mischievous, grubby children of an ill mother, cook and clean in a house invaded by death, give ear to the monologues of a harried person who desperately wants a listener, bear with the peculiarities of an upset acquaintance. The Passion of Christ is being hourly renewed in the sufferings of those about us. Are we blind to it? It is a waste of time to daydream about what we would have done for Christ had we been in Veronica's place. Veronica's opportunity is daily duplicated for us. "When you did it to one of the least of my brethren here, you did it to me."

men the possibility of pardon and grace. Hence his confession, his contrition, his absolution, his taking his pain as penance clearing away the temporal punishment due to sin, his promise of immediate entrance into paradise.

What of us when the disease, the disorder, the injury which kills the body, or the loss which withers the heart, sinks its talons into us? Do we say: "Free me from this or I renounce God"? Or do we say, with Dismas: "This is my due. I do not protest against it. If Christ suffered far worse, why should I furiously reject what has come to me? I accept it as the cross whereon I die. I ask that it be swallowed up in the cross of Christ. May I be with Him, may He be with me, in tortured time and in blissful eternity"? If this is our attitude, our intention, then we have won a victory before which all the heaped-up victories that this short-sighted, short-lived world celebrates are as a pinch of dust scattered by any vagrant breeze.

10

LOSS

On Calvary, where He is to be stripped of His life, our blessed Lord is first stripped of His garments. The rustic, well-worn cloak, tunic, sandals are removed. The soldiers, with their magpie instinct, claim them as booty. The last of His few possessions are thus taken from Him. He stands against the brazen sky all but naked.

The stripping is the culmination of a process which has been in train since the moment of the Son of God's conception in His Mother's womb. Of His becoming man we read in the Epistle to the Philippians that, being God, "He emptied Himself, taking the nature of a slave." This does not mean that He abdicated His divinity, ceased to be God. It means, rather, that He put aside the glory which is God's, renounced the honor due Him as God, to join us in our lowliness and our vulnerability, and to appear to us an ordinary mortal.

He had a Mother and a foster father. The latter died in the years of Christ's youth, a loss not without tears. The former He left, to walk the roads of Palestine, sow the seed of God's word throughout the country, arrange for the continuation of His ministry down to the bounds of time, and advance to His rendezvous with death. The familiar Nazareth was put behind Him, and the home He had loved and lighted with love.

He now had nowhere to lay His head, no roof to call His own. He ate what was given to Him. He had earned money as a carpenter, and had used it. But from money He had turned away. He and the Apostles had a common purse, but this He never touched. It was kept by Judas, and Judas "was a thief" who "took what was put into it." He had abandoned leisure, ease, the safety and satisfactions of a sheltered existence.

Yes, the process of stripping did not begin on Calvary; it was only concluded there. It characterized His whole life, as it must ever characterize the Christian life.

Christian or not, we find that, as the years slip away, we are stripped of so much, whether or not we would have it so.

Youth passes; the skin loses its freshness, the hair its lustre, the eyes their brilliance, the flesh its firmness, the muscles their suppleness. We are stripped of the bloom, the sheen, the attractiveness of springtime.

We may be stripped of health, or at least of vigor. Never a pain or an ache was once the rule with us. But the perfect functioning of the organism is impaired, and we fall victim to one or another ailment or a complication of disorders. At any rate, our physical co-ordination declines, our reflexes falter, we tire more quickly. We lose our teeth; our sight dims; our hearing fails; to breathe becomes a labor. We are stripped of mental powers: we become slow of mind, confused, perhaps even ill.

We are stripped of family, friends. We lose mother, father, husband or wife, and the heart is invaded by a sorrow which time mitigates but never dispels; someone is gone and with him or her a part of our being has been shut off, as an unoccupied room in a house is shut off. Sisters die, and brothers. Our children may go out of our arms over the borders of time. Neighbors move away into eternity. Our companions of schooldays, our friends of a lifetime, our associates at work take their leave. Each departure means an impoverishment. There is now no one with whom to talk over old times, no one to ask who it was that Mary So-and-so married, no one to share our memory of bibulous Uncle Billy or of Sister Aloysia who ruled the fifth grade. There is, too, the stripping involved in misunderstanding, estrangement, the waning of love.

We may be stripped of security. Once we had full and plenty; now we must count the pennies. We are stripped of happiness. Gaiety subsides like a spent fountain, and melancholy settles in with us like an unwanted, depressing guest.

The examples could be endlessly multiplied. We have cited enough to prove that life's progress involves a constant stripping away.

What a distressing thought! But it is the crystalline truth. For some it is insupportable. They cannot face it, cannot endure it. A glance at the alarming suicide rate indicates as much. For every one who, desponding, takes his life, there are many who drag out sunless days to the bitter end, many who sink into staring lethargy. Life, which once seemed so entrancing, so pregnant with promise, becomes an intolerable burden. Unless, of course, we have meditated on the stripping of Christ.

If we have, we know the meaning of what happens to us. His stripping was in preparation for the crucial work, the work of the cross; it was in preparation for His passage out of this world of shams and shadows to the enduring world of glorious Reality. He was going home to His Father through the doorway of death, thus freeing us from the death of sin. The things, the relationships of time could not be taken along, nor could they be allowed to hold Him back. In themselves, they availed nothing for His victory over death. They had to be removed, and so they were, ruthlessly, that He might go naked, possessionless, alone to the sacrificial altar and the portal of eternity.

We are stripped of beauty, strength, money and material goods, comforts and consolations, faculties of one sort or another, to impress upon us the fact that we are headed for a stark, supreme encounter which will issue in everlasting joy or everlasting agony. The issue will be decided by the state of our soul. At the judgment it matters not in the least that we were once notably comely or robust or wealthy or well thought of; all that matters is that we have adhered to God's will, seeking first His kingdom and regarding everything else simply in the measure that it would help us and others on to that kingdom.

Were we not so stripped, we might easily settle down in oblivion of the things of God. We might lapse into eating, drinking, growing fat, being merry—unto our damnation. There are many terrible words in the Gospel, but none more chilling, I think, than those of the Saviour which might apply to the irreligious people for whom all appears to go miraculously right in this world, those who suffer no obvious stripping: "Amen I say to you, they have had their reward." They will never

to others all save the modest minimum they must have to live on. Foolishness? No, wisdom. In both cases, there is determination not to be in thrall to mammon.

Again, there are people who sacrifice reputation. Their talents and opportunities are at least equal to those of others who attain dazzling fame and are looked upon by the masses of men as demi-gods. The people of whom I speak are content to do as good a job as they can and to be counted as nothing, forfeiting the celebrity and the acclaim which they might, by the self-promotion which is the disease of our age, attain. They remember our Lord's words: "When you have done everything that was commanded you, say, 'We are unprofitable servants; we have done what it was our duty to do.' "

Or, again, in this matter of reputation, there are those who silently bear misrepresentation and the losses this entails. They might easily clear themselves and confound traducers. But they seek no justification; they let the false image stand, knowing that God sees aright, that no one else's opinion matters, that the loss of esteem is to their inner betterment.

Such voluntary stripping is found in some form in the lives of all the saints. It appears to be a necessary condition of sanctity. Since all of us without exception are called to sanctity, voluntary stripping must have its place in our lives. We must not merely not grudge the losses of various kinds which come to us. We must also forego, or temper our use of, things which it is far from sinful to enjoy. In Lent we do this on a small scale: we give up candy, cigarettes, alcoholic drinks, the movies, and so forth. Lent, however, is but an eighth of the year. Is there to be no self-appointed penance during the bulk of the fifty-two weeks? Is our self-denial to be limited to a brief season?

Anyone with a keen Christian spirit realizes that the answer is a resounding "No." Throughout the year we must lead mortified lives. But isn't that a contradiction in terms? Doesn't the very word "mortified" mean "touched by death?" Yes, touched by the death of Christ. For us there would be no salvation, were not our lives touched by the death of Christ. Had He not secured for us the grace which empowers us to overcome evil and progress in goodness, our lives would end in eternal frustration. That grace He won by His death and all the circumstances of His death, including the literal and symbolic stripping He underwent. But the grace He thus won requires our co-operation. It will not save us in spite of ourselves.

Our lives must, then, be touched by the death of Christ in a second sense: namely, that we conform to it, that we strip away all which is at odds with His precept, counsel, and example, all which, in its use or abuse, distracts us from imitation of Him, all which places obstacles on the way heavenward—the way of the cross. We must strip away pride, that excessive love of self; anger, that irrational desire of vengeance; envy, that sickly sorrow over the good fortune of others; gluttony, that unreasonable use of food and drink; avarice, that idolatry of money; lust, that perversion, that hideous caricature of love, which makes venereal pleasure our chief good; sloth, that sluggish, bored disinclination to consider, much less do anything about, our spiritual welfare.

In short, we must be mortified in the exact meaning of the word, else we shall surely be, in the vulgar meaning, mortified at the judgment. We must strip ourselves in time or be stripped of our destiny in eternity.

11

DEATH

"It is appointed for every man once to die."
The commonplace so expressed by St. Paul ap-
plies to Jesus Christ no less than to any other son
of woman. Like us in all things save our sin, He is
like us in the necessity of departing this world
through the sundering of soul and body. He sub-
mitted to temptation, to grief, to hunger, to cold,
to fatigue, to pain. And now He submits to death.
There are those who say that death, not Christ,
died on Calvary. Such poetic speech is well meant,
but inexact. Death did indeed die, but only in a
figurative sense; Christ died in a very literal
sense.

On Calvary the vertical shaft of the cross was
set in the rocky hillock, the crosspiece was put
upon the ground. Our Lord lay on the earth
which was greening with new life, His arms flung
wide upon the lifeless wood. Through each wrist a
thick, wickedly pointed spike was driven by a rain

of hammer blows. A rope was passed across the Victim's chest, under His armpits and under the crosspiece, then over the top of the upright, and, with some soldiers pulling at its ends and others guiding the naked body, Christ was slowly, jerkily raised aloft. The two bars of wood were fitted together, then fixed together with more spikes, and the feet were nailed to a litle resting place on the upright. So do men dispose of their Maker and Judge.

All could now see the immemorial struggle between waning life and waxing death as renewed in the case of the Lord of life and death. The mob avidly drank in the sight of the Saviour in His last agony, sucking the juice out of each smallest detail. This was for them rare sport. Does anyone think that there could not have been morbid pleasure in the spectacle for the common people? All such a doubter has to do is to look at pictures in newspapers and magazines showing the expressions on the faces of a crowd out to see and to savor the death of a group of criminals before a firing squad. The death, and especially the violent death, of others fascinates our supposedly humane and compassionate kind.

The chief priests and their hangers-on strutted back and forth in the space about the crosses kept clear by the soldiery. By hook and by crook, by intrigue and by bluff, they had brought the man they hated to the brink of oblivion. They relished their grisly triumph, and sauced it with taunts and jests cast into the face which death was molding ever closer to the skull. "Save yourself," "Come down from the cross," they cackled in the presence of Love's immolation. He must not be allowed to die quietly; no, He must be riddled with invective so long as there was breath in Him. Yet He begged: "Father forgive them, for they know not what they do."

The soldiers were busy dicing over the only possessions of the dying Galilean. So inured were they to executions, so impervious to the special atmosphere of this execution, that they could squat upon the ground and play a game of chance.

At the foot of the cross was a small group different from the rest, a handful who felt sword-sharp sorrow and also a kind of surprising, surpassing exultation. It comprised the Mother of the Crucified, the Apostle named John, Magdalene from whom seven devils had been driven, and a few women who had assisted in the public ministry of Christ. The Mother, as we have said, knew the meaning of this sacrifice. She mourned the manner of its accomplishment, the suffering with which this Child of her womb was raked. But she perceived its necessity and what it would achieve. Though weeping, she was not desolate. Though grieved in heart, she was serene of soul.

And the others, in some measure, shared her dispositions. They joined then, as every man since has had the opportunity of doing, in the work of the world's redemption.

Death waited for three hours before claiming its Victim. It came upon Him, not in a rush, but as a slowly mounting tide, as a candle-quencher putting out rank upon rank of quivering flames one by one, as autumn chilling and stilling and blackening a garden little by little, blossom by blossom. He hung there against the disfigured day, His blood running out drop by drop, His fever rising to a rage, His wounds ever sharper and more searching in their bite, His senses withdrawing from contact with sight and sound and smell.

His attention, too, was loosed from His surroundings. He spoke to those about Him only twice. Once it was to the repentant thief. And the second time it was to His Mother and St. John: He gave her into the young fisherman's keeping, and the young fisherman into hers, thus symbolizing that thereafter, as Co-Redemptrix of our race, she was to be the Mother of all mankind. For the rest, He constantly speaks to His Father, quoting from the Psalms, repeating snatches of those songs of praise and petition which were so familiar to the Jew as to come almost unbidden to his lips in any situation. Finally, as the last convulsions stormed through His body, as His pain smashed to a killing climax, He cried: "It is consummated," meaning that His task was done, that He was signalling death to strike. And then: "Father, into Thy hands I commend my spirit," meaning that of His own will, freely and fully, He bowed to the divine decree and walked through the portal of death. As if in token of His being in command of Himself to the last, He slowly lowered His bruised, thorn-bound head, and all was over.

The death of Christ comes much closer to us, becomes much more significant to us, when we have seen others, especially our own kindred, die. And the deaths of others, especially our own kindred, are bearable if we have in meditation absorbed something of the mystery and the glory of Calvary.

A relative, a friend, lies upon his deathbed. The signs of the approaching end leap to the experienced eye. Fever has gone berserk, is racing to conflagration pitch. Hypodermics are administered, and you think of the nails. An icebag is placed on the head, and you think of the crown of thorns. An elevator door clangs, a tray is dropped, two strangers converse and laugh boomingly beyond the door, and you think of the indifference, the incomprehension surrounding Christ. You catch bits of a whispered conversation over by the window, and realize that it deals with the dividing of the dying person's possessions, and you think of the dicing soldiers. A little cluster of people close to the bed is saying the rosary, the litany, the prayers for the dying, and you think of that little cluster of people close to the cross. The dying person is so withdrawn, so absorbed in the climactic struggle, and yet there may escape a word, a phrase, a sentence which proclaims the triumph of Christ over the world, the flesh, and the devil— "Jesus," or "Dear Jesus," or "Sweet Jesus, have mercy on me," and you think of His prayer at the outer gates of mortality.

All this tearing apart of soul and body, all this breaking down and silencing of the organism, would be horrible were it not that He has gone before. There is no pathway of pain which He has not traveled ahead of us. And the most frightening pathway of all, the loneliest road, that which we must go each utterly by himself and which is swallowed up in impenetrable darkness and of which there is no readable report, this, too, He has traversed in advance of us. So that the horror is exorcised. To be sure, the body shrinks from dissolution; there is a sorrow in us at leaving our own, especially the helpless among them, there is a salutary fear in us of facing the judgment in which nothing is forgotten. But our spirit need not now quail and collapse before the masked face of death, since Christ has snatched the mask away and shown the nameless, paralyzing horror to be nothing other than going home to God.

To the pagan, death meant annihilation, completely ceasing to be, or it meant admission to some soundless, lightless, dreamlike, melancholy netherworld, where one was far less than when here on earth. To the Jew of the old dispensation, death meant transfer to a realm of shadows and gloom, a dingy and cheerless asylum for what remained of a man after the stilling of his pulse. For pagan and Jew alike it meant a diminution, a deprivation, a shrinking, a thinning, a dimming of the robust and vibrant life of earth.

But for the Christian the very reverse is true. "To die is gain," says St. Paul, and so say we all if we are the familiars of Christ. This is not to maintain that our temporal existence is unrelieved misery and that our attitude should be always grave or grim. The Christian spirit is the spirit of St. Francis of Assisi, seeing each day as an occasion of delight, seeing the world, for all its sin and pain, as so marked with the signs of God, so filled with the presence of God, so eloquent of the power and beauty of God as ever to lift up our hearts.

Yet our life is no more than a time of waiting and readying for what is to come: the summons home, the exchange of appearances for reality, the yielding of faith to vision, the possession of the God of whom we here have but hints, and the reunion in Him with those we have loved and lost. None of this would have been possible had Christ not died. None of this would now be possible did we not die. None of this would now be possible did we not die in the grace which His dying won for us.

"It is appointed for every man once to die." Our turn will come. It may be on the rainy highway, at the foot of a flight of stairs, in the unremembering sea, in a far city or in the place of our birth, among dry-eyed strangers or among our weeping relatives. Let us hope that it will be in a bed over which the Crucified watches, in the glow of candles symbolizing the Light of the world, with the murmur of supplication lapping us about, the Christ of the Viaticum within us, and the last blessing traced and lingering above us in the air we can no longer breathe. In any case, let us hope that, whatever the external circumstances, our inner state will be such as not to make Christ's dying not only of no profit for us but also the direst and most damning burden to be borne in hell throughout eternity.

The time to choose is now. Which Calvary is ours? Is it that of the chief priests and their sycophants—the Calvary of deliberate rejection of the will and word of God? Is it that of the shallow mob—the Calvary of superficiality and rootless opportunism and craving for mere excitement whether of miracles or of murder? Is it that of the bad thief—the Calvary of evil persisted in to the last and so binding and blinding in its grip as to prevent recognition and acceptance of salvation? Is it that of the soldiers—the Calvary of routine, brutishness, greedy materialism? Or is it the Calvary of the good thief, of Mary and John and Magdalene, of the One who on the central cross demonstrates life's central truth—that trouble and failure and humiliation and pain and death are, thanks to Him, steps not downward to nothingness, but upward to victory, to peace, to joy?

12

ESCAPE

The crowds had hurried home from Calvary, leaving it all but deserted. There stayed on from choice only Christ's Mother and a very few of His now fragmentary following. Soldiers and observers representing the chief priests reluctantly remained because the formalities required it. Two prominent and wealthy men, both members of the Sanhedrin, both secret partisans of the Saviour, took charge of the removal of His body to the tomb. The first of these was Nicodemus, who had once stolen through the night to find the Light of the world and to whom Christ had said: "This Son of Man must be lifted up . . . so that those who believe in him may not perish, but have eternal life." The second was Joseph of Arimathea, who had already prepared his own tomb, hewn out of rock, not far from Calvary and now offered it for the Saviour's resting place.

The two, probably inexpert in manual work,

loosened the nails and slowly lowered the limp, chill, pallid body. Tradition has it that our Lady received her Son upon her lap. In any case, she surely looked long at the still, blanched face. It is sometimes said that the face of one just dead has a peculiar, haunting beauty. You may know this to be true from experience. When the face is that of one of your own, how you gaze at it, how you search it, how it stirs memories of the past and speculations about that realm of mystery to which its owner has outrun you.

Did our Lady weep? She was human. But, much more importantly, she spoke to her living Son beyond the gossamer veil of death; she prayed with faith and hope and love.

The body was carried to the antechamber of Joseph's tomb. There it was washed, that terrain over which the battle of heaven and hell had raged, and which was scarred and pitted with the evidences of warfare. When one's father is laid out in death, one's glance falls on his crossed hands, signed with all his years of labor. That labor was done for others, for the sustenance of wife and children, for the maintenance of the sacred citadel of the home. How it stings one to look at those hands with their rude witness of a wordless dedication, an exquisite devotion which one could never requite. In a far greater measure does the body of Christ, marked from head to foot by the

Passion, stir one to realization of what He bore, what He did, to give us heavenly food, heavenly raiment, a heavenly home.

Narrow bands of cloth, saturated with ointments and spices, were wrapped about the body. A white napkin was fastened about face and head. A large cloth was arranged shroudlike about the entire figure. The body was removed to the tomb proper, where the thinned little company reverently saluted it. Then they withdrew, and an enormous rock, shaped like a millstone, was laboriously rolled into place to stop the mouth of the cave. The Maker of the earth was hidden in the earth. The seed had been buried in the ground.

This is the *"Ite Missa est"* of the first Mass. After it, all who attended that Mass were dispersed. Some, of course, had gone long since. They had never for a moment entered into the Sacrifice with understanding and love. Its whole meaning and impact and worth had passed them by. Hence it is inexact to compare them with those of us who needlessly leave Sunday Mass before it is over. At least we have some notion of what the Mass is, and doubtless have derived some benefit from it despite our inexcusably early withdrawal. Yet may there not be more blame and shame in our hurrying off for coffee, a cigarette, first chance at the morning paper, in our deliberately not sharing in the Mass to the last, than in the heedless herd's streaming away from Calvary before the finish of the action there?

What of the Saviour's Mother, of Magdalene, of John, of Nicodemus, of Joseph of Arimathea, and their few companions? When they turned from the barricaded tomb, they saw that night was about to enfold countryside and city. Day was flickering out, shadows were thronging into darkness. The small party of the faithful moved quickly through the dusk to the houses where they were occupants or guests. They left Calvary, yet they carried Calvary with them.

If it could be said of our Lady after the birth of her Son, after the angelic heralding in the winter sky, after the shepherds' eager pilgrimage to the monstrance of golden straw, that she "kept all these things, pondering them in her heart," can it not be said that the happenings on Calvary she also kept in her heart, pondering them? Obviously it can.

For her that first Mass had not ended. She renewed it in her mind, turning over and over its least details, every aspect of Christ's Sacrifice, every word He spoke during it. It would dominate, permeate, motivate her whole life thereafter. For her, it would affect everything, color everything, transfuse everything. It would be her sovereign point of reference, departure, return. So, too, in their lesser way, with those now clustered about her. For them the Sacrifice of the Cross would be the spring from which their lives would be fed, the north star by which their lives would be set.

What of us? Is the Mass for us the centre around which our life revolves? Does it rule and shape our being? Do our thinking, speech, conduct take their pith and tone from it? Or is the Mass completely left behind, dropped like a charred match, forgotten, once we leave church? Does the Action at the altar govern and pervade all our actions, or does it have no continuing practical influence on our day or week?

"Ite Missa est" does indeed mean that the celebration of the Mass is over. But it also means that now must begin the living of the Mass: in our steady advertence to God, in our prayer, in our treatment of others. The Mass is a dynamo from which there runs in uninterrupted flow the power for supernatural living in all circumstances. We must use it as such, or much of its significance and consequence is lost on us.

As Mary and the loyal few headed home, what was Jerusalem doing? It was preparing for the morrow. In a matter of minutes now, the Passover would begin. This was a principal feast, marking the Hebrews' release from Egypt.

For generations they had been held captive in an alien, pagan land. There they were harshly worked, ruthlessly exploited, used as less than human. They had longed, pleaded, groaned for liberation. If only they might get away, go home. But the hand of Pharao, heavy upon them, did not lift. A series of plagues had caused that despot temporary compunction, had induced him repeatedly to promise the Hebrews their freedom, but always, the plague over, he reneged.

Finally there came the historic night when the Hebrews were, by divine direction, to stand prepared for escape. They were to gather by families in their houses, dressed for a journey, staffs in hand, ready to move at a moment's notice. On the table there was to be a festal meal, the main dish a lamb, the blood of which was to be smeared on the doorpost. This was a sign that the household belonged to God's people, and was to be clemently passed by when, in the blackness, the angel of death ranged over all Egypt, snatching away the first-born in each dwelling, even Pharao's. The Hebrews obeyed the command, and as, on all sides, death struck the Egyptians and unmanned the survivors with fear and grief, the chosen people took to the moonlit road and made good their escape.

Ever after, on the anniversary of this prodigy, they and their descendants were to celebrate the Passover and the exodus from Egypt in solemn fashion, with each family reproducing the appointed meal in its own home and surrounding it with ceremony. It was this that the residents of Jerusalem and their visitors were about, as Mary, and the Magdalene, and John, and Nicodemus, and Joseph of Arimathea came into the silent, empty streets.

There is tragic irony here. Busy about the ancient ritual, at pains to do everything prescribed in commemoration of their remote forefathers' release from Egypt by God's intervention, these people thought nothing of what had been done that day on the now lonely little hill without the walls. They saw in it no more than the execution of an impious swindler whom their learned leaders had condemned. He had got His deserts; the grave had now cancelled Him; and that was the end of it.

Actually, that was only the beginning of it. Granted that Christ's body was fast in the tomb. It would not be there long, some thirty-six hours only. On the third day, rejoined to His human soul, it would step from the grave, resplendent. But we are not here speaking of the Resurrection. We are speaking of the period of burial.

No sooner was Calvary's sacrifice consummated than Jesus Christ descended into hell. We refer to this fact every time we say the Creed. What does it mean?

It does not mean a journey to the realm of the damned, of those who died steeped in mortal sin and therefore were forever, by their own choice, incapable of being in God's glorious presence. For them nothing could be done; the fruits of the Passion were unavailing, they had been refused. Rather, it means a journey to Limbo, where there awaited release the souls of those who, from Adam's descent from innocence until Christ's descent from the cross, had died unstained by mortal sin.

These, of course, were marked for heaven. But until the Redemption took place they could not be admitted to heaven. It was only after grace had been restored, and the keys to eternal life, that they could attain fulfillment. Meanwhile, these just men and women had to wait, some of them for centuries, like Moses, some of them for a relatively few years, like St. Joseph, in a place free of suffering but bereft of God's immediate and beatifying presence.

To that place of twilight the Son of God now comes. Joy breaks like the day. Limbo's populace is transported with delight. Their exile, their vigil, is over. They are at last to go home, not to the home which in Egypt the Hebrews had yearned toward, not to an imperfect, transient, terrestrial home, but to the Father's house in paradise. One after another they are touched by the Bringer of salvation—Elias, Isaias, Jeremias, Daniel, Ruth, Esther, Judith, the prophets, champions, paragons of the Hebrew people, and a new exodus begins.

The exodus from Egypt is being recalled in Jerusalem by people blankly unaware of the unspeakably greater and more marvelous exodus from Limbo. While an ancient, earthly escape is being commemorated in the city which rejected Christ, there is no suspicion of the tremendous escape being just then effected in eternity. These people cling to a figure, but the reality to which it had pointed and which immeasurably surpasses it, is unknown to them. They rejoice that their forebears were released from slavery to Pharao; they do not realize that this day they themselves have been released from slavery to Satan.

Are we inclined self-righteously to censure them? In their position we should probably have done no better. Indeed, in a comparable situation we may be doing much as they did. What are the divine favors which we cherish? That, with God's help, we escaped from debt, from an impossible obligation, from a humiliating predicament, from an engagement gone sour, from illness, from failure in an examination, and so forth. It is natural and proper that we should gratefully recall such instances of deliverance.

But what of the spiritual level? What of our release from original sin, our being freed of the guilt of countless actual sins, our escaping some evil habit, our getting away from some occasion of sin, some powerful and persistent temptation?

Do we thank God for these? The latter favors far surpass the former, just as the exodus from Limbo far surpasses the exodus from Egypt. It is much more important that the way to heaven be opened than that the way to the promised land be opened. It is a greater thing to come into the realm of grace and glory than to come into the country flowing with milk and honey.

Christ has brought us out of the house of bondage, out of the underworld of corruption, out of helplessness and hopelessness, and into the order of perfection and salvation. We must be ever aware of this. In consequence, our religion must not be that of mere external observance, the mechanical performance of a routine. Rather, it must mean aliveness to God and the things of God. It must mean love of God and the things of God, as well as love of the image of God wherever found. We must give God worship and service worthy of those set free and brought onto the supernatural plane. As St. Peter says: "You are a chosen race, a royal priesthood, a holy nation, a purchased people, that you may proclaim the perfections of him who has called you out of darkness into his marvelous light."

13

GLORY

"The curtain of the temple was torn in two from top to bottom; and the earth quaked, and the rocks were rent, and the tombs were opened, and many bodies of the saints who had fallen asleep arose, and, coming forth out of the tombs after his resurrection, they came into the holy city and appeared to many." Thus does St. Matthew describe what happened in Jerusalem when Jesus Christ died.

These intriguing details we generally pass over in considering Calvary and its aftermath. When the Saviour's side has been pierced, and the blood and water have cascaded from His heart, we, like the multitude, direct our attention elsewhere. Hence, we miss some of the most suggestive points of the narrative which does not stop with the stopping of the Sacred Heart, but runs straight through to the astounding developments of the morning of the third day.

The curtain of the Temple was rent, that curtain which shut the people off from the sanctuary. Its destruction was a symbol of the supersession of the old order: now there was a new covenant, and a new closeness, between God and men. Earthquake and the splitting of the rocks allowed nature itself, and especially this old and sin-steeped earth, dramatically to attest the breaking of the bonds of sin, the smashing of the ancient enmity between one world and the other, the ushering in of new days and new ways.

Most significant of all was the rising of the dead. St. Matthew is careful to underline the fact that this took place only after Christ's resurrection. It was not a case of ghosts being imagined by people distraught because of the unaccountable darkness which had shrouded the city when Christ mingled His last breath with the breeze. It was not a case of phantasms being imagined by people distraught because of the ominous heaving and groaning of the ground, which may have reminded some of words Christ had spoken to the Pharisees in a different context on Palm Sunday: "I tell you if these keep silence, the stones will cry out." No, here were no delusions.

This was something far different, quite unprecedented, something done to concretize and emphasize a tremendous truth: namely, that the resurrection of Christ was not peculiar and restricted to the Incarnate Son of God, but to be shared by all who, as saints (meaning friends and followers of the Saviour), had been one with Him in life. The conquest of death and the reunion of soul and body in glory—this is the destiny of all who, while in the mortal sphere, take Him as their portion and give themselves over wholly to Him. This is our destiny. When we are afflicted and downcast, we feel that our destiny is suffering and nothing else. What we must realize is our glorious destiny beyond the dark horizon.

We have alluded earlier to Christ's identification of Himself with us in His Passion. We have tried to show that what we find arduous and sometimes all but intolerable—for example, fear and guilt, suffering and humiliation, trials that drag on without resolution, and the certainty of death's snuffing the vital spark—all of them He took upon Himself. In part, He did so in order that, in these experiences, we might never be alone or uninstructed as to how to cope with them. And now He would have us see that, just as He partook of our pain in its many forms, so are we to partake of His glory. What happened to Him will, if we are faithful, happen also to us. And it will happen precisely because, in situations parallel to those He knew, we have done our best to imitate Him.

He rises from the dead in the very body which had been so sickeningly outraged. Now He is all radiance, all loveliness. But His flesh and bones are the very flesh and bones which, a few days earlier, had been blistered and bowed by the gales of hatred. This body which shines celestially is the body which cringed and shivered in the smothering shadows of Gethsemane. See agleam with undiminishing day the marks of the ubiquitous and relentless scourges. See like a crown of stars the traces of the crown of torment. See the joyful lustre of the spot on the shoulder where the cross rested like the weight of the world as He went to Calvary. See the brilliance of the great, ragged gaps in hands and feet where lodged the nails. See the incandescent beauty of the once ugly opening in the side, an opening still so real and so large that shortly a man will put his whole hand into it. The scars of agony are now like dazzling jewels. Just by looking at them you can read again the story of the Passion; they are not wiped out, obliterated, but transformed; nothing so stresses the story's surprising ending as do they.

This serves to remind us that heaven and its glory are won by things which in themselves may appear to have nothing to do with beatitude, things which may appear to be the very stuff of irredeemable wretchedness. Who, looking on Christ in the harrowing hours of Good Friday, would have thought that this could be the issue—

this splendor outrivaling a thousand clustered suns, this triumph beside which the sum of all others is puny and pale? Any seasoned and prudent observer would then have said, with ironclad assurance, that the Man from Galilee was headed for nothing other than the reeking trench in which the remains of criminals were thrown to rot unmarked and unmourned. But such a prediction, though it seemed absolutely certain, was dumbfoundingly given the lie by the event. The one who turned water into wine has now turned the black stream of temporal sorrow into a crystal torrent of everlasting ecstasy. It is not that one has been substituted for the other; it is that one has been turned into the other.

In the same way, all the trying and torturing things which fall to our lot while we wait in this anteroom of eternity will, if we take them as He did His Passion, be one day converted into measureless delight. Of themselves, they produce only defect and distress; of ourselves, we cannot make anything positive and potent of them. It is only through Him and with Him and in Him that they can become the glory which never ceases, never slacks. The anxieties which chafe our hearts, the reverses which keep us always off balance, the injuries done us, the scorn shown us, the illnesses which wear us out, the paroxysm which puts a period to our life, these are the unlikely threads of which is woven the happiness of heaven, provided that we place them in His pierced hands.

Or we may put in a somewhat different way the truth suggested by the stunning sequel to Calvary. Sometimes, sitting across the room from our mother in the evening while she is absorbed in reading or doing handwork, we get a chance to study her and note the ravages of time, work, worry. Perhaps on a nearby table is a picture of her in her youth. The difference is striking and saddening. The photograph, old-fashioned and fading, shows a slim, dark-haired, bright-eyed girl, with unlined face and smooth hands. Looking smilingly and eagerly into the camera, she seems to be looking confidently and expectantly into a future she is sure is full of wonders. Then we turn toward her as she is today; we see the wintry white of the hair, the dimmed eyes, the forehead wrinkled, the contours of the face altered, especially at the jaw, the hands thickened and reddened. We think of all that has wrought these changes, the passage of the years and decades, the ailing and failing of the flesh, the griefs that came sometimes in battalions, the unremitting round of work. And we think: If only she could be as once she was, if only clock and calendar could be turned back, if only the weathering and the sculpturing of time and trouble could be undone, if only this body which bore me and nursed me and has worn itself out for me could be restored to its youth.

It is an understandable wish, but vain. Or is it vain? Yes, in the sense of Gertrude's reproof to the brooding Hamlet:

> *"All that lives must die,*
> *Passing through nature to eternity."*

But not at all vain, when we listen to the trumpet notes of St. Paul's assertion: "This corruptible body must put on incorruption, and this mortal body must put on immortality . . . What is sown in corruption rises in incorruption; what is sown in dishonor rises in glory; what is sown in weakness rises in power; what is sown a natural body rises a spiritual body."

Life's battle scars are, so to speak, the raw materials which, in the resurrection, God will touch and turn into our badges of heavenly honor. The heroic survivor of military combat gets a medal; he is given a piece of metal attached to a piece of ribbon, in recognition of the wounds he has sustained. But in the resurrection it is our wounds themselves which become our evidences of distinction. A clever cheater can get hold of, and ostentatiously wear, almost any military decoration, although he has deserved none. But no one can by fraud achieve the glory of the resurrection, since this is simply the splendor of God alight in souls and bodies which have conformed, at any price, to the divine will. So that every sign of service which we regretfully observe in a dear one is but an assurance of greater splendor in the hereafter.

"Christ has risen from the dead," says St. Paul, "the first-fruits of those who have fallen asleep . . . As in Adam all die, so in Christ all will be made to live. But each in his own turn, Christ as first-fruits, then they who are Christ's, who have believed." That is a suggestive expression—"first-fruits." It means, in its literal application, the first of a crop to be harvested: the first corn from a field which stretches like undulant gold to the horizon, the first apple from an orchard comprising countless trees, the first grapes from a vineyard which marches up a sweep of hillside. All the rest will eventually be gathered in; all the rest will fare as the first. Hence, Christ, as the first-fruits of the resurrection, exemplifies what awaits each of us in all the crowding generations of men.

Our bodies are to leap into wholeness and vibrancy from the dust. Our souls are once more—and this time forever and inseparably—to be knit to those bodies. And all our woes and all our wounds are to be resplendent as were Christ's in the Easter dawn, are to be the gorgeous array, the wedding garments which admit us to the heavenly banquet. If, that is, we "are Christ's," if we "have believed" and lived our belief, especially in seasons of sorrow. Let this be our light through the sombre days of our years.